PARKER
PROSPERITY
PROGRAM

PARKER
PROSPERITY
PROGRAM

PARKER EDITORIAL STAFF

PARKER PUBLISHING COMPANY, INC.
WEST NYACK, NEW YORK

How to use the book
that builds your palace
of prosperity

TODAY—*now!*—YOU START TO BUILD
your Palace of Prosperity, a palatial mansion where you live like
a lord with fine possessions, a king-sized bankroll, personal honors
of every kind . . . prosperity so bountiful that even a titled lord
might envy it!

The nine Lessons in this book are nine blueprints—nine sets of
plans for the opulent rooms in your mansion of wealth. They give
you many mighty techniques of Prosperity Power. As a special
feature, they are written from several different viewpoints to help
you fit each great technique to *your* needs, build your own Master
Plan to fit *your* specific ambitions.

What treasures will sustain and fill your
Palace of Prosperity?

Anything you wish! Let your dreams soar where they will, because now you have the means to make your dearest dreams come

7

true! Surely *Prosperity* will mean money for the wonderful home you want to enjoy, a fine car, perhaps a country home too, fabulous vacations, the best of education for your children, expensive hobbies, the grandest of entertainment.

For many it will mean a job or business or profession of your own choice, where your newly-awakened abilities take you to ever-higher levels of prestige and top-bracket pay.

You can have a home life of glorious harmony, joyously shared with hosts of friends on a grand scale. Along with this, your prosperity can reflect itself in awards and citations upon which you proudly see *your* name cited for civic achievement or political standing.

Your Palace of Prosperity can include red-carpet treatment at the best hotels and restaurants—or a quiet retreat to faroff places where you can pursue cherished sports, or relaxation—or seasons of high living and seasons of quiet and worry-free rest.

And along with all that money can buy, you can enjoy a vastly increased measure of priceless energy and health! Your new self-confidence, your freedom from many worries and nervous tension, your prosperity-privilege of resting when you wish—all build your resources of well-being along with your resources of money.

Never before!—this Program which combines many lifetimes of experience with ageless wisdom and new scientific discoveries

Each lesson in the Parker Prosperity Program is based on a special prosperity technique or approach. In many cases, this technique represents a lifetime of research and study by some gifted man or woman. The techniques finally chosen represent the carefully-winnowed best out of more than one hundred suggestions. Each technique had to pass careful tests for practicality, ease of understanding, ease of use, and prosperity-building results which could be shown on the record.

You build your Palace of Prosperity quite rapidly—and "move in" very soon

Prosperity no longer need be an uphill struggle of ten, twenty, or thirty years! With the psycho-emotive tools and methods supplied in this completely coordinated program, you can build your Palace of Prosperity so soon you'll be wide-eyed in wonder! You may have an occasional setback. You will, of course, have to exert some effort and personal faith. But if you persevere, as I know you will, magnificent success will crown your efforts. You literally cannot fail!

To give you added help in many ways, you will find:

Personal X-Rays	consisting of self-analysis questions which make your growing prosperity more individually yours.
Checklists	for speedy scanning of key data about plans, potentials and ideals.
True Stories	which show how these nearly-magical Prosperity Methods worked for others and can work for you too!
"Q & A"	of which the questions came from many of the men and women who helped us pre-test, revise and perfect this Prosperity Program; thus they are likely to mirror questions which occur to you. Answers follow each question.
Special Devices	of great value in pinpointing your Prosperity needs and accelerating your Prosperity progress.
Psycho-Emotive Reminders	at the end of each Lesson, for quick review. Later, in your new prosperous life, you can check through the Psycho-Emotive Reminders for a quick brush-up every now and then, assuring permanent Prosperity.

Make this book your personalized, lifetime guide

Read with a pencil in your hand. Mark passages which particularly appeal to you. Fill in answers to questions where indicated. Make your own notes on each Reminder Page, where called for at the end of each Lesson. The more you personalize this Program, the more it will help you—first as you learn and practice the Prosperity Techniques—later when you review.

Now—start with Lesson One; "The Dynamic Laws of Prosperity." Watch confidently for a quick, startling increase in your Prosperity Power! Soon you'll move on to the other Lessons, putting up the sturdy structural frame of your Palace of Prosperity, then filling the rooms with your valuable new abilities and costly new possessions, then adding the final trim of Prosperity in Lifelong Happiness.

Start today!

ACKNOWLEDGMENT

Parker Publishing Company, Inc. gratefully acknowledges permission to include in the *Parker Prosperity Program* numerous excerpts and adaptations from the following books:

Catherine Ponder, *The Dynamic Laws of Prosperity: Forces that Bring Riches to You* (Englewood Cliffs, N.J., Prentice-Hall, Inc., 1962)

Napoleon Hill and W. Clement Stone, *Success Through a Positive Mental Attitude* (Englewood Cliffs, N.J., Prentice-Hall, Inc., 1960)

Frank S. Caprio, M.D. and Joseph R. Berger, *Helping Yourself with Self-Hypnosis* (Englewood Cliffs, N.J., Prentice-Hall, Inc., 1963)

William E. Edwards, *Ten Days to a Great New Life* (Englewood Cliffs, N.J., Prentice-Hall, Inc., 1963)

Roy Garn, *The Magic Power of Emotional Appeal* (Englewood Cliffs, N.J., Prentice-Hall, Inc., 1960)

Dr. Joseph Murphy, *The Power of Your Subconscious Mind* (Englewood Cliffs, N.J., Prentice-Hall, Inc., 1963)

Maxwell Maltz, M.D., *Psycho-Cybernetics: A New Way to Get More Living Out of Life* (Englewood Cliffs, N.J., Prentice-Hall, Inc., 1960)

Robert J. O'Reilly, *Dynamic Thinking: A Powerful New Shortcut to Personal Success* (Englewood Cliffs, N.J., Prentice-Hall, Inc., 1963)

J. V. Cerney, *How to Develop a Million Dollar Personality* (West Nyack, N.Y., Parker Publishing Co., 1964)

Parker Publishing Company also would like to acknowledge the special assistance of Monroe Schere in the compilation and editing of this work.

Contents

Lesson One: **THE DYNAMIC LAWS OF PROSPERITY   19**
"Money is divine" · The basic law of prosperity · The vacuum law of prosperity · The imaging law of prosperity · Can you attract money? · The prosperity law of command · The prosperity law of self-confidence · The prosperity law of prayer · Persistence

Lesson Two: **PROSPERITY THROUGH A POSITIVE MENTAL ATTITUDE   39**

The PMA way to set your goal and get there · Five rules of universal procedure · How to use PMA to motivate yourself and others · The magic motivating ingredient · The 13 self-motivators · To motivate others transfer your PMA · Can you attract happiness · The happiness-power of words

Lesson Three: **PROSPERITY THROUGH THE POWER OF SELF-HYPNOSIS   57**

The 4-A's method of self-hypnosis · Autorelaxation · Autosuggestion · Autoanalysis · Autotherapy · Self-

hypnosis and weight control · Nervous tension · Fatigue · Stay young, live longer with self-hypnosis · Posthypnotic suggestions · Prosperity Quotient Analysis

Lesson Four: **TEN DAYS TO A PROSPEROUS NEW LIFE   79**

Breakthrough and revealing actions that bring money · How to key your ideas to a single great purpose · Insight scrapbook · The as-if-ten-times technique · Your as-if form · Success is where you make it

Lesson Five: **THE MAGIC PROSPERITY POWER OF EMOTIONAL APPEAL   101**

Reach and command the minds of others · Self-preservation as an emotional appeal. · Four magic appeals · The magic of money as an emotional appeal · How to use romance as an appeal · Using recognition appeal to achieve success · Conversation secrets · Pack questions with emotional appeal · Prepare yourself for prosperity by relaxing with inward-directed emotional appeal

Lesson Six: **HOW TO MINE THE "MOTHER LODE" OF YOUR SUBCONSCIOUS MIND   121**

Your treasure is always with you in your subconscious · Exercises in subconscious choice · Practical techniques for mental healing · Your right to be rich · Free you of fear · Familiarity technique of overcoming fear · Your subconscious as your partner in success · How to become successful in buying and selling · Why grow old? · Prosperity Quotient Analysis

Lesson Seven: **PSYCHO-CYBERNETICS   141**

"Free throws" show the principle in action · Imagination and reality not far apart · Supply your guidance mechanism with direction · Prescriptions for developing personality · What is Psycho-Cybernetics · How to

unlock your best personality · Simple personality pep-ups that break the chains of inhibition · Nobody inhibits you except yourself · Three action rules · You can always change your mind about yourself

Lesson Eight: **DYNAMIC THINKING   163**

The one basic ingredient that separates the successful from the run-of-the-mill · Why is tomorrow-itis such a common disease · Question yourself about your own in-difference · How to get into the habit of doing it now · Where to find the time · Time categories · Time and success · Energy · An experiment in sleep · Dream and sleep research · Chart your sleep · Build your pro-ductivity · Push back your fatigue times · What suc-cess means to you · Rules of accomplishment

Lesson Nine: **HOW TO DEVELOP A MILLION DOLLAR PERSONALITY   181**

Personality is social seduction · Give or take estimation scale · Enthusiasm—your passport to a million dollar personality · The eight major ingredients of enthusiasm · Conversation questionnaire · How to make your con-versation project your best personality and do more for you · How to avoid emotional traps and expand your personality · Ways to predict how others will act · Your own healthy ego · Your human-relations IQ · Check your improved Prosperity Quotient

PARKER
PROSPERITY
PROGRAM

The Dynamic Laws of Prosperity

How to Handle the Forces That Make You Rich

Some people think it is wrong to be rich!

And yet it is *right* to be rich; *right* by every common-sense standard and by every standard of sensible faith as well. Russel H. Conwell, who was famous for his *Acres of Diamonds* lectures, gave us a guide of great motivating power:

> I say you ought to be rich, you have no right to be poor. To live and not be rich is a misfortune and it is doubly a misfortune because you could have been rich just as well as poor. . . . We ought to get rich . . . by honorable methods, and these are the only methods that sweep us toward the goal of riches.

To be truly rich means the same as being truly prosperous. It means having an abundance of all that is good, and the means to keep on having that abundance in a full, satisfying life filled with peace, health, happiness and plenty. This goal is your only proper goal; let no sense of inferiority or guilt keep you from attaining it! *Know* that riches are your goal, and riches become far more easy to attain than you may sometimes think.

"Money is divine," says this minister who has guided hundreds to riches

Catherine Ponder, a minister, worked out the Dynamic Laws of Prosperity which this Lesson gives into your hands. She remarks that few of us doubt that money is necessary. Most of us do not realize, however, that prosperity of all kinds is your *divine heritage.* Money protects you and your children from the soul-stultifying meanness and dangers of poverty; money lifts you onto a plane in which you can find and express your true talents, free your soul from excessive and worry-ridden toil; money gives you time for confident access to the spiritual plane of life through quiet contemplation, attendance at churches, participation in constructive endeavors made possible by money; money lets you LIVE amid all the comforts and luxuries and joys which God makes available to His children.

> During one of Dr. Ponder's famous lectures on Prosperity, one man almost fell out of his chair when he heard her say: "Money is divine, because money is God's good in its earthly expression." This man worked hard every day to make himself prosperous, yet he was not prosperous because he believed *money* somehow means *vice.* This conflicted thinking set up a conflicting result in his affairs, for what you want you must want whole-heartedly. When this man came to understand the *goodness* of money, he acquired money. His entire life, even his health, changed for the incomparably better.

Q: Should we not desire to be rich for the sake of the good we then can do for others?

A: *It is good to do good for others, but do not use this idea as a weak rationalization for getting rich—as though you really didn't* *deserve to be rich. Want to be prosperous because it is your right that you should be prosperous.*

Let us examine the Dynamic Laws of Prosperity which can make you prosperous through your own honest efforts, using the mind and the body God gave you, perhaps overcoming handicaps which have kept you back before—but now will give way as you claim your divine birthright!

THE BASIC LAW OF PROSPERITY

There is one major reason why poverty persists among people who are surrounded by opportunity and everything they need for a prosperous life. They do not give due credit to the Basic Law which says:

You must give before you can get.

Give what? In almost all cases, the most effective gift consists of your *faith* . . . shown in the right word, the right attitude, the right frame of mind! Often the value of a material gift lies in the *faith* behind it.

> A widow had no money in the house, not a bite to eat for herself or her children. "Give and you shall receive," she read in her Bible. What could she give? Prayerfully she asked guidance—and remembered flowers growing in her yard. She cut them and brought them to a sick neighbor, who blessed her for her thoughtfulness. Next, as though guided by an unseen hand, she spread a worn cloth on her table, causing her hungry children to dance with excitement. In simple faith, the widow now made out a grocery list for all the food she needed—but still did not have a dime to buy. Just then the doorbell rang. A man who had owed money to her long-dead husband dropped by and gave her $30 toward the debt which *suddenly, mysteriously,* he had felt impelled to pay. When the widow now invited him to stay for lunch, he was overwhelmed. He did all he could for that family, and now the widow has a good part-time job and the children are well cared for.

Often, the radiation of a sincere desire to cooperate with our fellow men is all that is needed to bring what we desire:

A stockbroker was depressed by the cries of alarm that surrounded him when the market began slipping. He went off by himself, relaxed, prayed awhile. He reaffirmed his resolve to deal honestly and openly with everyone he met; to treat every client as though that client were his own brother. He declared: *Everything and everybody prospers me now.* In a few moments the phone rang and it kept on ringing. Within a short time he had received more business by telephone than he had received through all channels in several days.

We are filled with pent-up substance, energy and divine ability which works for us, through us and around us. You release this pent-up power for prosperous living through radiating thoughts, feelings, prayers and mental pictures of success—sometimes modest success to fill an immediate need—sometimes all-embracing success to enrich the very source of your continued livelihood.

As you do so, your thoughts, feelings and mental pictures are radiated outward into the rich, powerful ethers of this universe, where they make contact with the eternally generous substance of divine intelligence and power. This universal substance then moves among and works through the people, conditions and opportunities which correspond to the rich radiations you have sent forth, and the prosperous results then appear!

All the prosperity laws given in this Lesson are various ways of invoking the basic Law of Radiation and Attraction, or, in plain words, the simple truth that you must give before you can get.

Now go on to the other Dynamic Laws of Prosperity where you will find more and more that is meaningful to *your* prosperity breakthrough, right now. Pause first, however, and murmur this quiet affirmation:

I am an irresistible magnet, with the power to attract unto myself everything that I divinely desire, according to the thoughts, feelings and mental pictures I constantly entertain and radiate. I am the center of my universe! I have the power to create whatever I wish. I attract whatever I radiate. I attract whatever I mentally choose and accept. I begin choosing and mentally accepting the highest and best in life. I now choose and accept health, success and happiness. I now choose lavish abundance for myself and for all mankind. This is a rich, friendly universe and I dare to accept its riches, its hospitality, and to enjoy them now!

THE VACUUM LAW OF PROSPERITY

Now we enter the realm of bold, daring faith! The Vacuum Law of Prosperity tells us: *If you want great and good prosperity in your life, start forming a vacuum to receive it!* This means: You get rid of certain possessions in the faith that you are thereby made more prosperous by far.

Q: Does that imply that I must give away my possessions after I have worked so hard to get them?

A: *It implies only that you should get rid of certain possessions you don't need, you don't really want, and which actually may be standing in the way of real wealth coming in. Some of these possessions may be material. Many will be unwanted emotional possessions—mental chains which hamper and frustrate you until you get rid of them and free your true prosperity power.*

If there are . . .

Clothes in your closet which no longer seem right for you; which really constitute a blight on your self-image . . .

Furniture in your home or office which, for the same reasons, should be replaced . . .

People among your friends or acquaintances who no longer seem congenial; who hurt you with their negative and discouraging influence . . .

Conflicts, grudges, areas of personal bitterness which for some reason have become precious to you so that you "nurse your wrath to keep it warm . . ."

Push this clutter out of your life! Do this in pure faith that you can have what you really want, and with a sense of adventure and expectation. When you create the vacuum, great beneficial forces find that vacuum and fill it in the way you desire.

A couple had to move. Fearlessly they gave away a great deal of old furniture and simply left bare spaces in their new home. They were very "broke," but they visualized the spaces filled with bright new furniture, and doubt never entered their minds. Then, *mysteriously,* this faith conveyed itself to the husband's employer, who gave the husband a wonderful chance to increase his income on a merit-point system. Money came in, and more: the husband won a number of prizes, one of which was a large choice of furniture!

The late Michael Todd gave us a saying which chimes in with this and every other proper, wealth-building attitude toward money: "I've never been poor, only broke. *Being poor is a frame of mind.* Being broke is a temporary situation."

A businessman grew very sick. It seemed that his body was filled with poison and nothing would dissolve it. Knowing the powerful effect of emotion on the body, this man decided there must be some mental attitude or emotional feeling which ought to go. He asked Divine Intelligence to reveal to him what he needed to release. Now he remembered that he had been holding a bitter grudge against a certain person and even had gone to great lengths to hurt this man. As he lay in the grip of a high fever, he declared quietly, over and over: *I fully and freely forgive you. I release you and let you go. That incident between us is finished forever. I do not wish to hurt you in any way. I am free and you are free and all is well between us.* For the first time in many nights he slept peacefully. The next morning his fever was gone, and his physician declared that the poison had miraculously left his system overnight.

Forgive—and good rushes in!

Forgiveness is the prime method of casting out the almost-literal devils of mind-poison which we so often cherish—to our lasting harm. Sometimes a grudge bites so deeply and lasts so long, it seems nothing can dislodge it. Yet forgiveness puts a lever under that mountain of bitterness, the mountain is moved, a vacuum exists, and forgiveness flows in.

A five-step forgiveness technique:

1. Take half an hour a day, for a few days, and sit alone or walk alone and think of those with whom you are out of harmony. Call them to mind firmly. See their faces.
2. As though they really were there, ask their forgiveness. If you

have discussed anyone unkindly, if you have quarreled with anyone, if you are involved in a legal or emotional tangle with anyone, mentally ask their forgiveness.

3. Watch for their response! At first it may be subconscious in a shy approach toward better relations; then ever more conscious and strong. Make it easy for them to approach you by being continually receptive and open toward them.

4. Mentally declare to others: *God's forgiving love has set us free. Divine Love now produces perfect results and all is again well between us. I behold you with the eyes of love and I glory in your success, prosperity and complete good.*

5. Include YOURSELF among those whom you should forgive! Do not go about with a load of guilt and self-blame weighing you down and casting shadows upon you. Declare to yourself: *I am forgiven and governed by God's love alone, and all is well.*

One man found forgiveness after a long struggle when he said: "Lord, I humanly cannot forgive that man, but if YOU can, please forgive him through me."

You never lose, you always gain through letting go of anything material or immaterial that is unwanted. In fact, you may never really know what you want until you move out what you don't want! Then your mind is freer, the world is brighter, your spirit is light and optimistic and confident, and the world's riches find you are ready to receive them.

THE IMAGING LAW OF PROSPERITY

Persist in picturing success! Nothing that is built upon this earth, nothing that is achieved, no great victory won but that it first was pictured in a human mind—and pictured greatly.

As a wise man said: "You are not merely a human being; you are a human becoming." Demand of yourself that you see with utmost clearness where you are going and what you want when you get there.

PERSONAL X-RAY

The following questions are a cross-section of the major desires which build a great life. Find an answer to each question which in any way applies to you. **Write down the answer.** Then think it over. X-ray yourself with searching honesty. Make sure you have not set down a goal which reflects a hesitant, frightened state of mind. You need big, golden goals to send forth the mighty vibrations which soon return with wealth, strength, fulfillment and all we wish for in our dreams.

My future in my personal life:

What would be the ideal living quarters for myself and my family?

What are my personal or family ambitions by way of education?

What grand good times do we want: vacation trips, for instance?

What do we desire to help us enjoy ourselves: a new car, a summer home, camping equipment, the best of hi-fi?

My future in my career:

Am I in the right job? Or the right kind of self-employment?

What kind of job do I really want?

Shall I stay in my present job but work for advancement—or seek another, better field?

What income do I need to achieve my goals?

My future among my fellow men:

What am I doing for my church? How much more shall I do by way of giving?

What have I done for my community? How much more shall I do, avoiding all excuses?

What have I done for my friends? For my neighbors? For strangers whom I meet? For my business associates? How much more shall I do?

Dr. Emerson Cady once wrote: "Desire is God tapping at the door of your mind, trying to give you greater good." If you suppress those deep desires, or tell yourself they are "impossible," they have no constructive outlet and may show themselves in frustrations, neurotic tendencies, alcoholism or other negative ways. Free your desires and they attract all you need to make them come true.

The father of a large family reported that he had about given up hope of being able to afford an adequate house for his brood. But when he wrote down a description of the house he wanted, it "came real." He found such a house for sale and affirmed to himself that he would have it. His faith reflected itself in his work, and he increased his income by 50% that year. He and his family now live in that house.

A lawyer had thought vaguely of expanding his firm from two-man size into five- or six-man size and entering into fields of greater service to others and greater prosperity for his partners and himself. He saw obstacles and at first let them discourage him. But when he wrote down his goal, he found himself dwelling on it, making plans, seeing that most of the obstacles were self-made (as most obstacles are). He felt the force of his desire carrying him along, guiding him. Now there are five partners plus a staff, and the firm has moved from a small office into spacious quarters which occupy an entire floor of a new building.

Of course we have to work to gain our goals. A better job, for instance, is not likely to come without investigation, perhaps special training, planning, seeing the opportunities which *you did not see until you really looked*. This preparation is part of giving. "Ask and it shall be given you; seek and ye shall find; knock and the door shall be opened. (Matt., 7:7, ASV)

Perhaps you are demurring that you really do not know what you want. In that case, simply make lists of attractive goals in all phases of your life. Go over the lists from time to time, adding or subtracting items, and the inner mind will make its own selection.

Even make lists of the things you want cleared up and eradicated from your life—for often the process will suggest the positive and powerful alternatives.

You always have used your imaging power.
Now use it constructively!

Yes, you have been *imaging* for most of your life—but perhaps you imaged *lack* of money, *lack* of success. Now put aside your inhibitions and take your wallet and your checkbook into your hands. Closing your eyes, image bills of large denomination bulging from your wallet. Image deposit slips showing thousands upon thousands of dollars deposited in your bank account.

Image, image, image all the good you wish to be yours! Your self-created image becomes a mould for the fluid forces of circumstance, a pattern which the Master Weaver gladly helps you follow!

THE PROSPERITY LAW OF COMMAND

Shakespeare wrote: "There is a tide in the affairs of men, which, taken at the flood, leads on to fortune." It is through the Law of Command that you release this flood-tide of good which you have built up through your list-making and mental images.

The secret of the Law of Command is this: *A positive assertion of the good you wish to experience often is all that is needed to turn the tide of events and produce good swiftly and easily.*

Command your good to appear!

No longer need you look "up" at life as though it were a mountain towering over your insignificance. The Law of Command helps you move up to the summit and look out over your world with a feeling of authority and control! To be in command, feel in command! Do this by making affirmative statements which carry you beyond all negative influences. Add to your confidence and powerful effectiveness by making definite declarations to meet definite needs.

If your money supply is low, do not dwell upon your lack but whenever you take your purse into your hands declare: *I bless you and bless you for the riches of God that are now being demonstrated in and through you.*

When you dress, speak in the words of one who has the fine wardrobe that comes to every prosperous thinker: *I give thanks that I am beautifully and appropriately clothed with the rich substance of God.*

The beautiful, comfortable home you desire comes closer to you in the web of circumstance as you declare in faith and joy: *I give thanks that I am beautifully and appropriately housed with the rich substance of God.*

And for the first-class transportation which every prosperous thinker should enjoy in an excellent car, or by plane, or on a luxurious ocean liner: *I give thanks that I am comfortably and appropriately transported with the rich substance of God.*

Recently a 40-year-old prospective mother asked for a positive statement of command when she entered the delivery room. Dr. Ponder gave her the statement: *God in the midst of me is mighty in life, health and strength. In joy and with ease I bring forth my perfect child.* Later the doctor told her it would be a difficult "breech birth" because the child was in the wrong position. Instead of becoming fearful, this woman continued to affirm over and over: *God in the midst of me is mighty in life, health and strength. In joy and with ease I bring forth my perfect child.* A little later the doctor reported in amazement that the child was changing its position. It was born normally and almost painlessly.

A man opened a restaurant and candy shop in a place where two previous owners had failed. His friends pointed out that the location was wrong, that times were bad . . . yet he made such a brilliant success, he soon opened two other restaurants. When asked how he had succeeded, he simply repeated the affirmation which had worked the seeming miracle: *I give thanks for the many customers whom I greet with love and good will, whom I am honored to serve with the best of food and the best of attention, whom I send forth with my sincerely spoken message of health and prosperity, and with my gratitude that they have shared with me a portion of God's bounty of money.*

Avoid hard times talk

Do not think, talk or act any way but prosperously. If you mix up your trend of thought, you set up cross-currents that confuse your efforts for prosperity. You should not become upset when others talk about hard times; neither should you join in their sad chorus. Instead, declare in perfect faith: *Divine restoration is taking place. The good which the locusts of lack have eaten is being divinely restored. The divine law of balance and equilibrium is doing its perfect work.*

Give yourself thought of increase

Dr. Ponder has noticed that many businessmen in her prosperity courses report positive benefit from the thought of *increase* as held in the mind and made dynamic by commanding affirmation. Along with affirmation, let your every act, tone and look express a quiet, rich assurance of success.

There are words which convince others of your success—and there is a radiation beyond words, a feeling of richness implanted in your mental atmosphere. It is then radiated from you and subconsciously communicated to others. They will want to be associated with you in business transactions. They will want to be your customer. They will want to be your friend. They will feel themselves benefited by the feeling of richness, success and prosperity that you radiate.

PERSONAL X-RAY

> X-ray some situations which lie ahead of you. Are you going to meet an important client? Are you going to sit down and talk things over with a young person who isn't "on the ball"? Are you going to have an operation or meet some other emergency?
>
> X-ray yourself as you see yourself *typically* handling that situation. Watch for evidence of the Prosperity Law of Command. Do you see it? If not, start now to affirm to the inward mind that truly guides you: *I thank God for my strong command of the success-forces in the situation ahead*—name them, such as confident ability to show the other person your love for him and your interest in his prosperity; or complete faith in the Divine Hand that in time of trouble is held out to take yours—*and for my ever-growing competence in living my good, healthful, prosperous life.*

Always affirm *love* in your dealings with others. To those close to you, affirm your love openly and often. Especially should you affirm your love when the other person is in doubt or pain, or perhaps has made a mistake or done something he should not have done. Love can be an exchange of strength between two people, or strength shared in a family group like a bounty from an overflowing table.

Outside your immediate circle, love becomes *brotherly love.* Assure others of your interest, approval and sincere appreciation of them. A public relations director for a worldwide insurance company says that, in his work with thousands of employees, he has found that their greatest need is kindness. Command over others—so necessary if you are a boss—can be a part of simple brotherly love and thus evoke hitherto-unseen powers of prosperity.

You become what you want to be by affirming that you already are

There is no easier or more delightful way than daily affirmation and command to get you onto the royal road to success. Here too, you can and should write out your favorite affirmations. Keep them where you can be reminded of them—perhaps in your pocket or purse, or pasted onto your mirror. One man writes his affirmations on a cardboard book-mark which he uses constantly.

Here is a three-step formula which gives remarkable results. Follow these three simple steps and open the floodtides of *good* in your life:

1. Daily write out your affirmations of desired good.
2. Mentally image the successful results.
3. Boldly and deliberately affirm and command those successful results to appear.

THE PROSPERITY LAW OF SELF-CONFIDENCE

A psychological researcher reported that he had studied the question of prosperity from every angle, had observed many prosperous people, had read many biographies of those who prosper; and from all this he decided that if the key to prosperity could be described in one expression, it would be: SELF-CONFIDENCE.

PERSONAL X-RAY

Sit with yourself and find your own honest answer to this critical question:

Does your self-confidence come *after* you have succeeded? That is, is it a kind of negative self-confidence, in that you have to succeed before you allow yourself to believe you are capable of succeeding? Or . . .

Do you believe beforehand in the inevitability of success, so that success comes to you with a joyful feeling that you have, *of course*, fulfilled yourself?

Real self-confidence is not an afterthought! It is as much a part of you as is your breathing. Self-confidence in its fullest sense means:

1. Innate, unquestioned faith in one's abilities and talents
2. Faith in God's unwavering help in showing the way to use your abilities and talents to their fullest and most powerful extent

Actually, you *have* self-confidence. The Psalmist reminds us that you were made a little lower than the angels, and crowned with glory and honor. You have not only self-confidence, but every other divine quality which can build the kind of life you want to build.

Notice this in children, who have a delightful self-confidence until, alas, some outward influence sows the seeds of fear and doubt. Go to an exhibition of paintings by young children and see how amazingly good they can be, in their delightful unsophistication . . . before the child learns that painting is "hard" or "takes years before you can be good, if ever." Think of the many cases in which children lost in the woods survive where adults perish—because the child has not learned to be afraid.

A Sunday School teacher, realizing this, leads her children in affirmations of self-confidence. It is wonderful to see how these children blossom forth as adults who enjoy life and have a great record of successful living.

Quite different is the case of a man who was extremely inhibited about prosperous thinking—couldn't "let himself go"—but tried it, stayed with it, and soon felt its lifting power in his increasingly successful affairs. Then a friend laughed at him for his affirmations and he gave them up. Very soon his entire life started going downhill. He was wise enough to stay away from this person thereafter and seek the help of a counselor who once again gave him faith in himself and faith in faith . . . with notably successful results.

Build confidence thoughts before sleeping

Psychologists believe that your last waking thoughts are the ones on which your subconscious mind feeds and acts while you sleep. If you fill your mind with happy, expectant thoughts of success and prosperity, your subconscious will take them as orders from you. During sleep, your subconscious will obediently go to work to produce a prosperous tomorrow.

Link yourself with self-confident people

Just as your own thoughts and attitudes affect others, so do the thoughts and attitudes of others affect you. Check the general level of optimism among your associates. You may find you are hurting yourself by absorbing daily doses of pessimism at lunch, or with your car pool, or from your neighbors over the fence. Make yourself aware of these influences, and, if you cannot avoid them, erect the barrier of your self-confidence against them.

Better yet, associate with success-minded, self-conscious individuals. They will subconsciously inspire you and lift you to higher levels of thought and expectation. Perhaps Jesus was thinking of the power of self-confidence when He said: "If I be lifted up, I will draw all men." (John 12:32)

Let your self-confidence draw forth the good in others

> A commercial photographer is a great success in photographing prominent models in the fashion world. He says that his success comes as a result of expressing to those models, before he takes a picture, his confidence in their ability to photograph well. He says that this transferral of confidence makes the girls radiant before the camera. Few retakes are necessary, and he does twice the work in half the time.

Refer back to the Personal X-ray on Page 31 and you'll see this is the same principle at work. To give confidence to a person who is struggling to succeed, don't wait to see his hard-won success. Anyone can say: "John, I'm proud of you, but I knew you could do it all the time." Share the magic power of self-confidence at the time he needs it. Let it give him the big boosts toward success that it always will give you.

THE PROSPERITY LAW OF PRAYER

"Prayer is profoundly simple and simply profound."

Thus a man who had not prayed for many years described the way in which prayer came back into his life, to stay with him thereafter.

> Along with his friends, this man was a "hard-headed businessman." He had not gone to church, nor prayed, for many years. He fell ill, and for a time lay close to death. When he recovered, he found that many of his "hard-headed" friends had prayed for him. He thereupon admitted that he had prayed for himself. Weak and half-conscious, he had prayed to the Unseen and somehow had felt that other voices were raised in prayer—the voices of those who, knowing him, somehow were attuned to his own mind. This man and his friends now are humbly thankful they broke through their self-imposed barriers of cynicism, for the blessing of prayer has stayed with them and has vastly enriched every part of their lives.

Side by side with the other prosperity laws discussed in this chapter, the power of prayer cannot be over-emphasized as a factor in permanent, satisfying prosperity. Yet many people do not employ the power of prayer because they have an erroneous idea that it is wrong to ask for something when you pray.

It is right and just that you should pray for whatever you may need, yet you should realize there is a "divine selection" in what your prayers bring to you. In the words of Emmet Fox: "Prayer does change things. Prayer does make things to happen quite otherwise than they would have happened had the prayer not been made."

Four kinds of prayer

First, there is general prayer. General prayer is praying to God as a loving, understanding Father in your own private way. It can be on your knees or in any comfortable position. It can be with a prayer book before you, or it can be by browsing through the Bible, dwelling upon favorite passages. General prayer generates spiritual power. Like love, it need not be particularized, but is in itself a sustaining force, an ever-ready source of comfort and strength.

Then there are prayers of denial. They help you to reject things as they are, to dissolve your negative thoughts about them and make way for something better. Prayers of denial help you to erase what is not true and right; help you to be free from less than the best in your life.

> A man who came out of prison, truly reformed, feared what people would say behind his back. When this fear came upon him, he used the prayer attributed to Daniel in the lions' den: *My God hath sent his angels and shut the mouths of the lions.* He soon found that the doubting attitude of others was replaced by their respect.

Prayers of affirmation are the third type. Following upon prayers of denial—as though filling the vacuum—they bring in the firm, new good you desire.

> A man who had gone into bankruptcy used prayers of denial to rid himself of the same kind of inferiority and shame which had haunted the ex-convict. Then he prayed affirmatively for frank, honest courage with which to face his creditors, found it, and found out they were quite willing to talk things over. He received more help than he had at first thought possible, got back onto his feet, paid his debts and restored both his business and his good financial standing.

Finally there are prayers of meditation and silence. It is often in meditation and in silent, contemplative prayer that you feel the presence of God's goodness most strongly. In this type of prayer you take a few meaningful words and think about them and feed upon them silently. Gradually they grow in your mind as expanded ideas that move you to right action, or perhaps as peaceful assurance that all is well and no action is needed. If nothing seems to happen in meditation, you have nevertheless made the mind receptive to God's good and, at the right time, ideas and opportunities will be revealed.

The great lesson is that it is possible to solve problems by quiet, relaxed meditation, rather than by fighting them. You should take time daily for quiet meditation. It strengthens and confirms your knowledge of yourself and of others, helps you realize the full lessons of your past and how to apply them to your future, helps you win ever-closer contact with the eternal source of your spiritual power.

There is one more Law of Prosperity. It is *Persistence.* Just as the basic Law of Attraction and Radiation underlies all others, so is persistence required in the application of all laws. Persistence is a universal ingredient of success; yet also, alas, it can be turned toward determined failure. Know that your patience and energy now will carry you ever forward, upward, onward, as you expand the Dynamic Laws of Prosperity into pillars of lifelong strength.

Psycho-Emotive Reminders:

It is divinely right for you to be rich! Cast aside all mistaken notions that there is anything wicked about prosperity, or that it needs to be excused. Honorable methods help you win a good share of God's bounty of money.

The basic law of prosperity shows us why we must give before we get. All other laws build upon this great truth of radiation and attraction.

The vacuum law of prosperity requires bold faith in getting rid of material possessions which do not suit your prosperity-image; and emotional possessions, such as grudges, which hamper your prosperity power.

The imaging law of prosperity gives you mental images of terrific strength. Confidently you image success, large sums of money, anything you want, knowing it can and should and will become real.

The prosperity law of command gives you key affirmations which command the aid of mighty forces. Even your love of your fellow men adds to your command-power to win a prosperity-filled destiny.

The prosperity law of self-confidence gives you a major secret of victory—unquestioned faith in your own abilities and talents; also the amazing secret of sharing self-confidence with others.

The prosperity law of prayer explains the four ways of prayer which make prayer your positive ally, helping you think more clearly, understand more quickly, change your life in a grand upward sweep, day by day.

My Personal Notes on Lesson One:

Suggestions:

Watch for ways in which you already use the Dynamic Laws of Success, in whole or in part. Write down those ways, each on a separate sheet of paper, and staple those pages to this page, where you always can find them.

Beneath each Law, from time to time, write the ways in which you have strengthened the operation of that law in some important area of your life.

Record any story, "Q & A" or Personal X-ray which had special meaning to you. Do this throughout the book, and you form a priceless pattern of self-revelation.

Don't let these suggestions limit you. Make as many notes as you wish, on as many extra pages as may be necessary. It is an excellent idea to use pages of book-page size so you can keep them neatly in the book.

The next Lesson presents the experience of two men who came through "the school of hard knocks." Today, along with great happiness and fulfillment, they measure their success in tens of millions of dollars. These two men now give you the success method they followed and point out exactly how you can follow it too.

Prosperity Through a Positive Mental Attitude

How to Awaken the Sleeping Giant of Your "PMA" and Blaze Your Way to Success . . .

"WE ARE POOR—NOT BECAUSE OF GOD!"

PSYCHOLOGICAL RESEARCHERS, MINisters, and self-made businessmen come to the same conclusion: We are poor or rich not because God ordained it but because of the way in which we use the talents and abilities given to us by God!

S. B. Fuller started work at the age of five, the son of a poverty-stricken Negro farmer who expected nothing more than a life of gruelling want. But Fuller's mother said: "We are poor—not because of God. We are poor because we have not developed a desire to be rich." Young Fuller decided he would be rich. For twelve years he sold soap from door to door. In those years he saved $25,000, hoping to buy a small company. Then he found out that the company he worked for could be bought for $150,000. He said he'd buy it, put down his $25,000 as deposit—to be forfeited if he could not raise $125,000 within a certain time—and went out to raise money. Although he was almost unknown, his positive mental attitude brought him loans till he had $115,000. The night before the deadline, with every credit resource exhausted, he knelt and prayed to God to lead him to a person who would lend him $10,000.

That night he saw a light in the window of a man whom he knew very slightly. He walked in and said: "Do you want to make $1,000? Lend me $10,000 now and when I bring back the money, I'll bring back another $1,000 in profit." He left with a check in his pocket. Today he owns four cosmetic companies, a hosiery company and a newspaper.

What the mind can conceive, the mind can achieve

S. B. Fuller started life under a cloud of *Negative* Mental Attitude far deeper than most of us meet. Choosing a big goal, finding his *Positive* Mental Attitude, he acquired the strength he needed to overcome every obstacle. He acknowledged the help of God in sustaining his faith—and God helped him through his Positive Mental Attitude.

Napoleon Hill and W. Clement Stone, the two businessmen who have built Positive Mental Attitude into a mighty success method, point out that what the mind can conceive, the mind can achieve. Think of a magic talisman in the shape of a coin, with PMA (Positive Mental Attitude) engraved on one side and NMA (Negative Mental Attitude) engraved on the other. With great achievement firmly set in your mind, the PMA side of your talisman does not turn up merely 50% of the time; it turns up 99% of the time!

The PMA way to set your goal and get there

Your day has 1,440 minutes. Invest one percent of that time in a study, thinking and planning session and you will be astounded at how those 14 minutes help you know the best side of yourself and feel the mighty dynamics at your command. During one or several of those sessions, do this:

1. Write down your goal. The very act of thinking as you write creates a deep impression in your memory.
2. Give yourself a deadline. Like S. B. Fuller, you will rise to the occasion.
3. Set your standards high. Those who ask life for pennies get pennies. Those who ask for riches find a definite relationship between the strength of their motivation and the ease with which they achieve their high goal.
4. Write down the first step to take and resolve to take it NOW. Confirm yourself in the habit of immediate action. When you delay as a form of self-indulgence or unwarranted fear, you encourage your subconscious mind to make you a constant waster of priceless time and opportunity. DO IT NOW and your subconscious mind is encouraged to make you a doer, an achiever, a winner.

Here is a mighty advantage you gain when your goals are clear-cut and fully visualized: You become alerted to opportunities which present themselves in your everyday experience and you always are in a position to ACT NOW.

Edward Bok, an immigrant boy, told himself he would become a writer and run a magazine. He picked up a picture of a famous actress, one of a series which was packed with a brand of cigarettes, and noticed its reverse side was blank. His alert mind filled this side—with the actress's biography! He went to the firm which printed the pictures, explained his idea and was promised $10 apiece for 100-word biographies of 100 famous Americans. Before long, Bok had five journalists busy turning out biographies while *he* was the editor. Later he became the famous editor of the *Ladies Home Journal.*

Yet the picture of an actress would have been nothing but a picture to someone who did not know his goal and fuel it and fire it with PMA!

You have a problem? That's good!

Why is it good to have problems? Because repeated victories

over your problems are the rungs on your ladder of success. With each problem solved you grow in wisdom, stature and experience. You become a bigger, better, more successful person every time you tackle a problem and conquer it with PMA.

PERSONAL X-RAY

Make a searching list of victories you have won in your adult life. These may include job advancements, big sales, winning any kind of contest, achieving any goal in any area. (These need not be big victories, so long as they carried you ahead of where you were before.)

Now examine each item and remember the problem you solved before your victory was won. Of course you solved a problem; otherwise you could not have won your victory!

It takes only one idea, handled with PMA,
followed by action, to win where others fail

In 1939, on Chicago's North Michigan Avenue, office space was going begging. You could look right through many a building because it had so many empty floors. NMA hung in a black cloud over Chicago real estate offices. All you heard was: "No sense in advertising, nobody has money to pay rent." "What can you do? Nobody can fight bad times." Nobody but a man with PMA can fight bad times!

One man had a giant office building on his hands with one-tenth of its offices occupied. But—he said, "I have a problem? That's good!" He saw it as a challenge. He reasoned that if the offices went unrented they produced no income, so it was worthwhile to invest in attracting tenants. He sought out desirable tenants and offered to assume responsibility for their present leases if they paid him the same rental under a one-year lease. He offered redecoration without cost, offices superior to most. To make sure the offices were attractive, he employed the best creative architects and interior decorators.

The result was marvelous. The tenants became so enthusiastic that they spent additional large sums on remodeling. At the end of a year, the building was 100% rented. It maintained a high percentage of rental, because when a tenant had to move he always offered a warm recommendation—and it's easier to rent space in a building that's nearly full. So the "white elephant" building turned into a money-maker, while up and down the street dozens of buildings still stood practically empty because "Nobody has money to pay rent."

Time after time the pattern repeats itself: problems and difficulties turn out to be the best things that could have happened to us—provided we scrutinize them for their advantages, using the mighty view-clearing power of PMA.

Realizing that some people can use PMA's problem-solving potential more readily than others, Mr. Stone and Mr. Hill worked out a universal procedure which anyone can use in any problem-situation:

1. Meet your problem with faith. Reach out beyond yourself. The first element of the PMA success method—*It is not because of God that we are poor*—reminds you that God is a good God, giving into our hands the means of success if only we will use them. Ask, therefore, for divine guidance. The sincere attunement to forces beyond yourself is one of the most positive and powerful actions of the human mind.
2. State the problem. Analyze and define it. For instance, is your problem to buy a suitable heavy coat to keep you warm? Or is your problem *to keep warm?* When the basic problem is clearly seen, you can explore many avenues for a solution.
3. Think. The solution is in your mind but has to come forth. Frantic nudging may drive it deeper. Think quietly, think with faith about solutions for your problem.
4. State to yourself enthusiastically: "So I have a problem? That's good!"
5. Ask yourself, and answer, as many specific questions about that problem as you can. Explore such matters as: people involved, viewpoints involved, money involved, help available for certain courses of action, who else has solved the problem and how, have I met a similar problem in the past? Ask every question you can think of. Turn the problem inside-out and upside-down, always with faith that the answer is close to your hand. This climax-step of the entire five-step process soon reveals how that which seemed to be a liability can become a mighty asset.

HOW TO USE PMA TO MOTIVATE
YOURSELF AS WELL AS OTHERS

Q: What is really meant by motivation?

A: *Motivation is an emotional slant which induces action of a certain kind or determines choice. We may say it is an inner urge, of a strictly individual nature, which, in response to certain stimuli, causes a certain person to act in a certain way. Meanwhile, of course, another person may react to the same stimulus in an entirely different manner. Here are the ten basic motives which inspire all human action:*

> *The desire for* **self-preservation**
> *The emotion of* **love**
> *The emotion of* **fear**
> *The emotion of* **sex**
> *The desire for* **life after death**
> *The desire for* **freedom of body and mind**
> *The emotion of* **anger**
> *The emotion of* **hate**
> *The desire for* **recognition and self-expression**
> *The desire for* **material gain**

When you know principles which can motivate you, you know principles which can motivate others. Conversely, when you know principles which can motivate others, you know principles which can motivate you.

Is there a magic motivating ingredient?

Some years ago, a successful cosmetics manufacturer retired at a ripe age. His friends always had asked him to disclose the secret by which he motivated women into buying his products, but half-jokingly he always had refused to tell. Now, however, he said he would reveal the secret.

"I never promised any woman that my cosmetics would make her beautiful," he said. "But with every package or jar I always gave her HOPE."

Hope is the magic motivating ingredient!

Hope applies to any product, any service.

Hope is a desire plus the expectation of obtaining what is desired plus the belief that it is obtainable. A person consciously reacts to that which, to him, is desirable, believable and obtainable. Hope is a key ingredient of your Positive Mental Attitude—provided you back it with courage, strong desire and unbounded faith!

Can we hope to free ourselves completely of PMA?

Realistically speaking, you should not desire this so long as PMA is your general pattern. Certain negative thoughts and feelings are good—in their proper place. They become a necessary defense against strong negative powers directed against us by others.

Consider *anger* and *hate*. Righteous indignation against evil is a form of anger and hate. So is the desire to protect one's loved ones or one's nation against attack by an enemy. Sometimes we may use the most drastic and irreversible form of negativism, killing, to accomplish a worthy purpose.

Consider *fear*. Every new experience and every change of environment may bring with it some shade of fear, however slight. This is Nature's way of protecting you from potential danger. You may think you are not sufficiently brave; yet some tinge of fear, or at least of caution, comes to the bravest person at some time. The person with PMA, however, quickly will understand his fear, then neutralize it with his own positive approach to the new condition.

How to motivate yourself toward becoming the kind of person you want to be

Are you among the millions who have read the *Autobiography of Benjamin Franklin?* This great book contains a motivation method that sparkles with wisdom and power.

Franklin first listed 13 precepts (we might call them self-motivators) which he considered necessary for a good, happy, successful life:

1. TEMPERANCE: Eat not to dullness; drink not to elevation.
2. SILENCE: Speak not but what may benefit others or yourself.
3. ORDER: Let all your things have their places; let each part of your business have its time.
4. RESOLUTION: Resolve to perform what you ought; perform without fail what you resolve.
5. FRUGALITY: Make no expense but to do good to others or yourself, that is, waste nothing.
6. INDUSTRY: Lose no time; be always employed in something useful.
7. SINCERITY: Use no hurtful deceit, think justly, and, if you speak, speak accordingly.
8. JUSTICE: Wrong none by doing injuries, or omitting the benefits that are your duty.
9. MODERATION: Avoid extremes, forbear resenting injuries so much as you think they deserve.
10. CLEANLINESS: Tolerate no uncleanliness in body, clothes or habitation.
11. TRANQUILITY: Be not disturbed at trifles, or at accidents, common or unavoidable.
12. CHASTITY: Rarely use venery but for health or offspring, never to dullness, weakness, or the injury of your own or another's peace or reputation.
13. HUMILITY: Imitate Jesus and Socrates.

Franklin went on to say: "Conceiving that . . . daily examination would be necessary . . . I made a little book, in which I allotted a page for each of the virtues. I ruled each page with red ink, so as to have seven columns, one for each day of the week, marking each column with a letter for the day. I crossed these columns with thirteen red lines, marking the beginning of each line with the first letter of one of the virtues, on which line, and in its proper column, I might mark, by a little black spot, every fault I found upon examination to have been committed respecting that virtue ,upon that day."

Here is one of Benjamin Franklin's charts:

	S.	M.	T.	W.	T.	F.	S.
	TEMPERANCE						
	Eat not to dullness; drink not to elevation.						
T.							
S.	●	●				●	
O.	●●	●	●		●	●	●
R.			●				●
F.			●				
I.			●				
S.							
J.							
M.							
C.							
T.							
C.							
H.							

Now make your own list of ten or a dozen motivating virtues which have special meaning to you. To make such a list is in itself a revealing experience, for it shows you the major characteristics of *the person you want to be.*

Your list probably will not be the same as Franklin's. Read his list again, however. Notice how his "precepts" parallel the generally accepted moral teachings which make civilization possible. Franklin began his career as a poor boy, with little beyond some pieces of bread in his pockets. Those highly moral precepts helped him become highly prosperous and one of the most influential men of his world.

Here is the essence of Franklin's formula, which it will pay you well to follow:

1. Although you remain aware of your entire personal list of motivating virtues, concentrate on one principle for an entire week. Keeping it in the forefront of your mind, respond by proper action every time an occasion arises.
2. Start the second week with the second motivating virtue, and so forth. Your week's work with each will allow it to be taken

over by your subconscious mind. Should an occasion arise when the employment of a previous principle flashes into your conscious mind . . . ACT! DO IT NOW! This is a tremendous reinforcement for your prosperity habits.

3. When the series is completed, start over again. Thus in a year you will complete the cycle four times. Long before that year is up, you will feel the strength of your self-motivation and the tremendous influence it gives you in motivating others.

To motivate others, transfer your PMA

Napoleon Hill was another who started his life under a black cloud of NMA. The motherless boy was always in trouble. His father and his brothers kept on telling him he was bad, and this only confirmed his own negative view of himself as a hopelessly bad person.

Then a stepmother was brought into his life. His father introduced him as "The worst boy in the hills." But the stepmother said with sympathy and understanding: "Not at all! He's the brightest boy in these hills, and all we have to do is to bring that out in him." From that moment on, young Napoleon tried to make himself the kind of boy his stepmother had faith he would be.

There is no doubt about it: PMA can be transferred from one person to another. Faith such as that possessed by Napoleon Hill's stepmother is highly *active*. Active faith steps out on its belief and assumes it will succeed.

When you motivate others by having faith in them, then *you* must have an active faith. You must commit your belief. You must say: "I know you are going to succeed on this job, so I have committed myself and others to your success." When you have that kind of faith in a man, he will succeed. When you have that kind of faith in yourself, *you* will succeed!

To be enthusiastic, act enthusiastic

Ways to motivate yourself and ways to motivate others constantly overlap each other. The motivating force of *enthusiasm,* for instance, almost automatically is conveyed from one mind to another. Enthusiasm is an all-important part of selling anything to anybody.

You may not be a salesman, but you "sell" more often than you may think. You "sell" your likes and dislikes and your wishes for certain action to other people—and your confident enthusiasm gives you a great deal of influence and control.

The great secret of becoming enthusiastic is: Act enthusiastic! Emotions are not immediately subject to reason, but they are subject to action—for better or for worse. Let us look in on a school for salesmen. The instructor's words are in regular type; the student's answers are in italics:

Q: Do you want to feel enthusiastic?
A: *Yes.*
Q: Then learn the self-motivator: To be enthusiastic, act enthusiastic. Now repeat the phrase.
A: *To be enthusiastic, act enthusiastic.*
Q: Right! What is the key word in the affirmation?
A: *Act.*
Q: That's right. Let's paraphrase the message and thus you will learn the principle and be able to relate and assimilate it into your own life. If you want to be sick, what do you do?
A: *Act sick.*
Q: You're right. If you want to be melancholy, what do you do?
A: *Act melancholy.*
Q: Right again! And if you want to be enthusiastic, what do you do?
A: *To be enthusiastic—act enthusiastic.*

The instructor then points out that you can relate this self-motivator to any desirable virtue or personal aim. Thus we might take *honesty* as an example, and say: *To be honest, act honest.*

Coming back to enthusiasm, the instructor gives six important rules for conveying enthusiasm through the all-important tool of speech. Remember these rules whenever you wish to persuade another person into some action which you fervently wish him to accept:

1. *Talk loudly!* This is particularly necessary if you are standing before an audience with "butterflies in your stomach."
2. *Talk rapidly!* Your mind functions more quickly when you do.

3. *Emphasize!* Emphasize words that are important to you or to your audience. The word *you* is always an important word.

4. *Hesitate!* When you talk rapidly, hesitate where there would be a comma, period or other punctuation in the *written* word. Thus you employ the dramatic effect of silence. The mind of the listener catches up with the thoughts you have expressed. Hesitation after a word you wish to emphasize accentuates the emphasis.

5. *Keep a smile in your voice!* Thus, while talking loudly and rapidly, you eliminate gruffness. You can put a smile in your voice by putting a smile on your face, a smile in your eyes.

6. *Modulate!* This is important if you are speaking for a long time. You can modulate both pitch and volume. You can speak loudly, yet intermittently change to a conversational tone and a lower pitch.

A three-barreled story

W. Clement Stone has inspired many people with a story he tells about his own experience in training salesmen. This story has a three-barreled effect; it shows the motivating power of faith, a "mind-conditioning" method of solving problems and the power of motivating by example.

Mr. Stone listened to a salesman explain that he could not sell accident insurance in his Iowa territory because the people were very clannish and would not buy from a stranger; and besides, the entire territory had had a crop failure for five years. Mr. Stone asked the salesman to drive him out to the territory. During the ride, he sat with closed eyes, relaxed, meditated and conditioned his mind to see the *advantages* instead of the obstacles the salesman had seen.

If you sell to the leader of a clan, you can sell to the entire clan! As for the crop failure . . . good! Those clannish people came of solid, thrifty stock. They'd want to protect their families and property. Probably they had not purchased accident insurance in a long time because salesmen were not even trying to sell in that territory, so there was no competition!

Mr. Stone now repeated to himself with reverence, sincerity, deep emotion and expectation: "Please God, help me sell! Please God, help me sell!" Then he took a nap. When they arrived in the territory, they called at a bank. Within 20 minutes the vice president of the bank had purchased a big policy. Then, going from store to store, office to office, Mr. Stone sold the same big policy to everyone he interviewed. Quietly and sincerely he pointed out that nobody knows when trouble may strike—as these people well knew—and how little it cost to insure that bills would be paid if an accident should happen. While riding home he thanked Divine Power for the assistance he had received. But without the PMA which turns problems into opportunities, he would not have seen *why* that group of people were ripe for accident insurance, and exactly *how* to go about selling it to them.

The salesman returned to the same territory and stayed a long time. Each day was a record day in sales for him. But this was not all. He never forgot the ways in which Mr. Stone had shown him how to turn negatives into positives. Today he is not only a far richer man but far more serene and confident in his entire approach to life.

Can you attract happiness?

Abraham Lincoln once remarked: "It has been my observation that people are just about as happy as they make up their minds to be."

The big difference between one person and another is *attitude* . . . positive or negative *attitude*. People who want to be happy will adopt a positive mental attitude and be influenced by the PMA side of their talisman. Thus happiness will be attracted to them. Those who consistently turn up the NMA side, however, repel happiness. Lincoln was one of many who sensed this great truth.

Remember an old song!

An old popular song declares that the singer wants to be happy—but he won't be happy till he makes the other person happy too!

Here is a secret of happiness which forever eludes those who spend endless money and time in a search for "thrills" and for elaborate possessions, but end with a feeling of emptiness in their lives. Yet *giving*, rather than acquiring, often is so much simpler—and *giving* gives a basic happiness.

The wife of a professor in the religion department of a large

university remarked that for some years they lived next door to
a very old couple who were not the best of neighbors. Noticing
that the old people were not getting around very well, they decided to fix up a small Christmas tree for them, and they took it
over the night before Christmas. The old woman, nearly blind,
cried with joy as she gazed dimly at the sparkling tinsel. Her husband, confined to a wheelchair, said over and over: "But it's been
years since we had a tree!" In a little while both the old people
were gone, but the deep, warm memory of their happiness has
remained to give happiness to those who gave it.

There are those who think they are not happy unless they are
constantly suffused with a feeling of joy; but this *euphoria* comes
close to being insanity when it is too long continued. The most
blessed kind of happiness is, rather, a state of basic contentment.
You will have some ups and you will have some downs, but your
basic contentment assures that you generally will be happy. Always,
the determining factor is the influence of your positive or negative
mental attitude.

Happiness begins at home

In one of the PMA Science of Success classes a very gifted, aggressive young man declared: "I have decided to leave home!"

When he was asked to discuss his problem, it developed that he
lived with his mother and neither was happy. The instructor realized
that the mother had an aggressive, dominant personality similar to
the son's.

The class was informed that any individual's personality can be
compared to the powers of a magnet—in two ways. First, each of
us has a personality-magnetism which strongly attracts the good
things of life if we develop its power. Second, our personality-
magnetism either can line up with that of another person's, and
push in the same, harmonious direction; or the two magnetisms may
oppose each other, thus causing conflict.

The instructor told the young man: "Your behavior and your
mother's are so similar that you can determine how she reacts to
you by the way you react to her. You can therefore, solve your
problem by applying the following rule of PMA:

"*When two forceful personalities are opposed and it is desirable that they live together in harmony, at least one must use the power of PMA.*

"Here is your assignment: When your mother asks you to do something, do it cheerfully. When she expresses an opinion, either agree with her pleasantly or don't say anything. When you are tempted to find fault with her, find something good to say. *She will probably follow your example.*"

"It won't work!" said the student.

"It won't work with an NMA approach," said the instructor, "but you can make it work with a positive mental attitude."

A week later the young man reported that in giving his mother pleasant cooperation, he had evoked in her a pleasant cooperation which seemed to have been "waiting to be born." He had decided to stay home. He liked his home now.

The happiness-power of the words we say

Regardless of who you are—you are a wonderful person! Yet certain other people may not think so, and this becomes most obvious and most painful when they are people in your own home.

Check what you say and how you say it! The voice and words often reflect the mood and attitude of the mind. The friction you find with other people may reflect the friction they find with you. Give them the good you want to receive from them!

If your feelings are frequently hurt by what others say, try to determine the true reasons for your *hurt* reaction; then avoid causing the same reaction in others.

If you are not happy when someone yells at you in an angry voice, think what you do when you yell at another person—even if it is a mischievous five-year-old.

If you feel offended because another person misunderstands your intent, show your confidence; give the other person the benefit of the doubt.

If sarcasm or humor with a personal sting offends you, assume such approaches are not pleasing to others and set them aside, along with gossip, as negative qualities you do not want.

And if you like to be complimented—if you like to be remembered—if it makes you happy that someone thinks of you—remember to remember others and let them know how important they are in your life.

There is nothing mysterious or revolutionary about PMA

A positive mental attitude depends on such well-known positive characteristics as faith, hope, charity, optimism, cheer, generosity, tolerance, tact, kindliness, good-finding, initiative, truthfulness, straightforwardness, and good common sense. Can these "old-fashioned" virtues get you anything you want out of life? Yes, they can and they will—when your PMA focuses your life in the way you want it to go.

Psycho-Emotive Reminders:

What the mind can conceive, the mind can achieve! If you are poor, it is not because of God. Conceive your great goal of riches and happiness and you can attain that goal through the magic of PMA—your all-important Positive Mental Attitude.

Every problem you solve is a rung upon your ladder to success. It takes only one idea, handled with PMA, followed by action, to succeed where others fail. A five-step procedure can be applied to any problem, turning obstacles into advantages.

PMA can motivate both you and others to achieve mightily and so win the best in life. Benjamin Franklin showed that key motivations of high morality and self-discipline can lead to prosperity and to personal effectiveness of a high degree. You can use his method.

To be enthusiastic, act enthusiastic! A salesman's lesson gives us a life-lesson in the power of action upon the emotions, and the transfer-power of emotions as a key to influencing others.

You can attract happiness! By giving happiness you win happiness. By acting toward others as you wish them to act toward you, you evoke mighty, beneficial results.

PMA is based on all the well-known positive character-istics of life, helps you use these characteristics with firm confidence while you win the kind of life you want.

My Personal Notes on Lesson Two:

Suggestions:

Bearing in mind all you have learned, watch for the ways in which people use PMA and NMA. Notice how the same situation will cause a negative reaction in one and a positive reaction in another. Keep a record of the ten most dramatic instances you can find, and change this record as you see better instances.

Think of some big problem-area in your life. Write down how you could have handled your affairs better in this area. You need not be entirely "practical," but can let your mind adventure into many possibilities. Some will seem possible after you write them down, even though they did not seem possible before.

As you did previously, record any story, "Q & A" or Personal X-ray which had special meaning to you. Cor-relate these items against all others previously set down. You are beginning to understand more and more about the wonderful person who is YOU.

The next Lesson gives you modern methods for using a remarkable tool of self-improvement: *self-hypnosis.* You see how to use self-hypnosis to relieve tiredness, nervousness and mental depression—how to give yourself post-hypnotic suggestions for accomplish-ment—how to develop new thought patterns that help you build a richer life.

Prosperity Through the Power of Self-Hypnosis

An Astounding New Technique for Freeing the Latent Powers of Your Mind

To HELP YOU IN GETTING AC-quainted with the techniques and benefits of self-hypnosis, remember this: You have already used your self-hypnotic powers hundreds or thousands of times!

Whenever another person irresistibly persuaded you—whenever you made an "impulse" purchase—whenever you became so emotionally involved in a piece of fiction or drama that you felt you were living the characters' lives—you practised a kind of self-hypnosis. True, the influence came from an outside source; but *all* hypnosis is self-hypnosis. The most expert hypnotist merely gets his subject to hypnotize himself.

Do not be afraid of the word *hypnosis*. Rather, make friends with the idea and you can turn it into a wonderful and valuable aid in living a prosperous life. Any form of self-hypnosis really is a form of *psychic healing* accomplished through the *voluntary acceptance and application of one's own suggestions*. Notice that the suggestions are *your own* and that you *voluntarily* accept them. Nobody, including yourself, can hypnotize you against your will!

FACTS AND FALLACIES ABOUT HYPNOSIS

Fallacies	*Facts*
A hypnotist has mysterious magic power.	A hypnotist (including yourself) merely has learned the art of effective suggestion.
A hypnotized person may remain "under" a long time and be hard to arouse.	The hypnotic state is similar to becoming completely absorbed in a movie or a novel. The hypnotist or the subject can terminate the hypnotic state at will.
Many people cannot be hypnotized.	Ninety per cent of all people can be hypnotized. The ability to be hypnotized successfully lies within yourself.
You can be hypnotized into doing anything, good or bad.	Under hypnosis you will not do anything improper nor anything against your moral principles.
You have to be in a deep stage of hypnosis before it can help you.	Many great life-improvements have been obtained in a state of light induction.
Only weak-willed persons are easily hypnotized.	The more intelligent and imaginative you are, the more easily can you be hypnotized.

Fallacies	*Facts*
Being hypnotized means lapsing into unconsciousness.	Being hypnotized, even in a deep state, still leaves you aware of everything that is going on.

Your authorities and teachers in self-hypnosis are Dr. Frank S. Caprio and Joseph R. Berger. Dr. Caprio is a practising psychiatrist who has written more than a dozen books on medical, psychiatric and related subjects. Mr. Berger is a psychologist and counselor, widely known as a writer and lecturer on psychology and hypnotism. This lesson presents their method of self-hypnosis as worked out for personal, private use. It is a method already used by hosts of people in several different countries to help health, get rid of fears and tensions, win specific benefits such as the ability to control weight and to quit smoking. It can remake your personality in any way you wish—help your life go in any direction you wish it to go.

Decide what you want self-hypnosis to do for you

Your conscious mind is critical; it judges the information your senses bring to it, and sometimes may judge wrongly or put up barriers against action. Your subconscious mind, however, is not critical. Once you "reach" it with a firm command that takes root, that command will govern you.

To understand your problems at the conscious level is a prerequisite to understanding, handling and solving them at a subconscious level—the level you reach with self-hypnosis. You must therefore ask yourself some pointed questions.

The following 15 questions are typical, and some probably will fit you. Take them mostly as suggestions, however. In the right-hand column, fill in 15 more questions they suggest to you. (This is not a questionnaire.)

PERSONAL X-RAY

1. Do I have an inferiority complex?   16. ....

2. Do I have a distorted sense of values?

3. Am I overweight?

4. Am I "difficult"?

5. Am I jealous?

6. Do I smoke too much?

7. Do I want to give up smoking completely or cut down?

8. Do I manage money wisely?

9. Do I suffer from excessive shyness?

10. Do most people like me?

11. Am I a hypochondriac?

12. Do I dislike myself?

13. Am I too fearful?

14. Am I too sarcastic?

15. What is my major personality handicap?

17. ....

18. ....

19. ....

20. ....

21. ....

22. ....

23. ....

24. ....

25. ....

26. ....

27. ....

28. ....

29. ....

30. ....

Q: Am I limited to 15 extra questions? I can think of dozens!

A: *Write down as many as you wish, using the book margins or an extra sheet of paper stapled to this page. Fifteen is a handy number, about right for most people. If you have a long list, go over it later and try to combine several questions into one.*

Once again you can see the value of *goals*. Most of your goals in self-hypnosis will be highly personal and concentrated, at least at the start. You may proceed to the actual techniques of self-hypnosis and practice them before you set up definite goals. Meanwhile, the preceding list helps you think about them.

THE 4-A'S METHOD OF SELF-HYPNOSIS

The Caprio-Berger method of self-hypnosis consists of four steps. You will recognize the prefix *auto,* meaning *self.*

1. Autorelaxation
2. Autosuggestion
3. Autoanalysis
4. Autotherapy

The first step: Autorelaxation

It is encouraging to note that many researchers have found deep relaxation possible with essentially the same technique.

Select a room where you will not be distracted. Subdue the lights. You may wish to play soft music. Lie down on a comfortable couch, or sit in a semi-reclining chair and place your feet up on a hassock. Loosen any tight clothing.

Take three deep, slow easy breaths. Close your eyes. Say quietly within your mind:

"I am going to relax all the muscles of my body . . . starting from my head to my feet . . . The muscles of my face and neck are relaxing . . . relaxed. . . . The muscles of my shoulders and my chest are relaxing . . . relaxed. . . . I'm feeling free of all muscle tension. . . . My arms feel limp and relaxed, limp and relaxed. . . . The muscles of my thighs, feet, legs are relaxed. . . . . As I breathe deeply and slowly my entire body is completely relaxed. I feel calm and relaxed, calm and relaxed all over. . . . "

During this state of self-relaxation remind yourself that relaxation is a *state of mind.* It means relief from anxiety and tension, freedom from excessive fear and worry—thinking pleasant, soothing thoughts. Tell yourself also:

"Self-relaxation will bring me inestimable health benefits. I am going to devote as much time and effort as I can to practising the technique of self-relaxation. If I don't succeed immediately I am not going to get discouraged. Each time I practise self-relaxation, it will be easier."

The rapid method of Autorelaxation

While you are practising the ordinary method of Autorelaxation, find some key word or phrase which is of especial help to you. It may be on the order of *Let go,* or *Calm yourself,* or merely *Relax,* or even the name of a relaxed person or of something which invariably makes you relax, such as the sight of a *kitten playing.*

After a week or two, all you may need is the key word or phrase to send you into deep, restful relaxation. Condition yourself to certain action along with the word or phrase. This may be the drawing of three slow, deep breaths, closing your eyes, suggesting that all your muscles from head to feet are suddenly as limp as though you were a rag doll. You can relax completely in a minute or two.

Now practise achieving *instant* relaxation with your eyes open, while walking, sitting, even driving a car. You will remain completely aware of your surroundings and in full control of your actions, yet you will be in a state of inner receptivity to self-induced suggestions. Once you have achieved this state, congratulate yourself for having achieved an important first step in self-mastery.

The second step: Autosuggestion

Hypnosis works on the theory of *suggestibility.* Your goal is the voluntary acceptance of a self-suggestion which is important and meaningful to you.

Here is a suggestibility test you should practise. In a little while you will feel a greatly increased receptivity to suggestion.

Pick out a spot on the ceiling or some other object above eye level, so that to look at it puts a slight strain on the eyes and eyelids. Count slowly to ten, without strain, and try to get your eyelids to droop and close at the count of ten, as though of their own volition. If you experience an irresistible urge to close your eyes on or before the end of the count, you are in a state of heightened suggestibility. This eye closure test requires you to be quite relaxed.

These suggestions can help you. Do not memorize the exact words; only their form is important:

"As I complete the count to ten, my eyelids will become very heavy, watery and tired. Even before I complete the count of ten, it may become necessary for me to close my eyes. The moment I do, I shall fall into a state of self-hypnosis. I shall be fully conscious, hear everything and be able to direct suggestions to my subconscious mind. *One* . . . my eyelids are becoming very heavy . . . *Two* . . . my eyelids are becoming very watery . . . *Three* . . . my eyelids are becoming very tired . . . *Four* . . . I can hardly keep my eyes open . . . *Five* . . . I am beginning to close my eyes . . . *Six* . . . my eyelids are closing more and more. . . . *Seven* . . . I am completely relaxed and at ease . . . *Eight* . . . it is becoming impossible for me to keep my eyelids open . . . *Nine* . . . my eyes are closed, I am in the self-hypnotic state . . . *Ten* . . . I can give myself whatever posthypnotic suggestions I desire."

The third step: Autoanalysis

Begin with self-relaxation. Follow this with the eye closure procedure. Then give yourself the suggestion that you now are ready to solve your specific problem. Whatever it may be, analyze every aspect of it as you sit or lie in a comfortable state of undisturbed self-hypnosis. Regress far back into the past. Try to associate the events and circumstances in your life which led to the development of your particular problem. Ask yourself some of the questions you previously listed, or any new ones which may occur to you. Perhaps:

SELF-HYPNOTIC PERSONAL X-RAY

What kind of person am I?
How is my health affected by the way I think?
To what extent am I oversensitive?
Do I really want to improve myself and the life I live?
What plans have I made for the future?
Am I inclined to blame my parents and others for my deficiencies?
What is my attitude concerning sex, love, marriage?

Take one or two questions at a time and try to think of as many possible answers as you can. You'll be amazed at the insight you gain, and how much more clearly you see yourself when, with self-hypnosis, you put aside many thought-inhibitions.

When you awaken yourself from your hypnotic state, write down the answers to your questions. Study carefully what you have written and try to reach some conclusions as to why you think and behave as you do.

Keep a sheet of notepaper which you can move from Lesson to Lesson in this book. Rule a line down the middle. Label one side: WHAT I HAVE LEARNED ABOUT MYSELF. Label the other: WHAT STEPS I HAVE TAKEN TO IMPROVE MYSELF. You will find that your mind soon becomes *conditioned to self-improvement*. The more you give it, the more it will want!

The fourth step: Autotherapy

Self-therapy consists of conditioning your mind to a positive plan of action through the use of post-hypnotic suggestions. That is, you give yourself orders, while in self-hypnosis, which later you will follow with complete confidence and a high proportion of success.

Self-therapy requires several sections for its discussion. You will find these sections in the remainder of the Lesson, and you will be able to concentrate on those which have especial value to you.

First we shall clear up some important points:

1. *How to rouse yourself out of the hypnotic state*

    After you have completed giving yourself posthypnotic suggestions, you can tell yourself that at the slow count of ten you will arouse. You *will* arouse, and with a feeling of great emotional well-being, inspired by the knowledge that you are going to benefit immensely from your self-hypnotic session. Nobody ever has failed to arouse from hypnotism.

2. *Any emergency will "snap you out of it" instantly*

    Hypnosis is not unconsciousness. You always are aware of your surroundings. Should you smell smoke, or hear a cry for help, the hypnotic state will automatically be interrupted. Your instinct of self-preservation always is stronger than your hypnosis.

3. *Certain physical and emotional ailments should not be self-treated*

    Hypnosis can do away with a great deal of pain and discomfort. First, however, you should allow a competent physician to make sure that a pain in the abdomen, say, is not caused by appendicitis or some other serious condition.

Similarly, hypnosis can relieve even serious nervous tension and anxiety. Yet, if such tension or anxiety arises from some deep-seated emotional cause which should have professional attention, be sure you get that attention.

SELF-HYPNOSIS: THE MODERN APPROACH TO SUCCESSFUL WEIGHT CONTROL

Self-suggestion in reducing weight is a scientific aid which has gained increasing acceptance and use by many physicians. No "miracle diet" can help you get through to your subconscious mind and make up your mind in the only way it can be permanently "made up." Excessive eating, like any other bad habit, *can* be controlled or broken by the power of self-suggestion. Movie actress Connie Stevens had this to say: "As soon as you make up your mind to be thinner, you can. I used to cut myself a large slice of cake every time something went wrong and I got upset. Now when I feel like doing that, I laugh at myself and say, 'Oh, no, that habit is broken!'"

Not all people overeat because of emotional problems. Regardless of the reason for overweight, the use of self-hypnosis is one of the best answers to the problem. Here's how to take off those extra pounds that slow you down, tire you out and constitute a definite health hazard.

1. When you have mastered self-hypnosis, use it to tell your subconscious mind that you fully intend to do something about it and *get results.*
2. While still in hypnosis, give yourself the post-hypnotic suggestion that you'll go into partnership with your physician. Simply tell yourself in so many deep, relaxed thought-words that you are going to take a "physical" to find out how reducing will affect you in regard to any possible blood-pressure prob-

lems or the like. Also you will get your physician to help you set up a calorie count and determine what calorie reduction is best for you and how best to go about this.

3. Establish a proper motivation for losing weight. *Health* is fine, but don't forget *appearance, ability to qualify for a job,* or whatever else may apply.

4. Make a list of the foods you can eat and cannot eat, and memorize that list. Repeat self-hypnosis with special attention to the foods you should not eat. Tell your subconscious mind you do not want these foods, nor too much of any food. See yourself saying *no-thank-you.*

5. Keep a weekly progress record of your weight. Make a chart. See the weight curve come down. At certain points, say when you have lost ten pounds, reward yourself by buying a new dress or a new pair of trousers in a smaller size.

6. Repeat daily in your self-hypnosis sessions that you now have developed new eating habits, you no longer are susceptible to temptation, *your mind is in control at all times.*

Using self-hypnosis to get rid of much nervous tension, pain and fatigue

In an article in *The Washington Post,* it was reported:

> So enthusiastic has been the acceptance of medical hypnosis by the medical profession that it is estimated more than 10,000 doctors, psychologists, psychiatrists and dentists . . . are using it in their daily practice. The positive results are phenomenally high. (The figures are as of 1960.)

The article cites the case of Mr. M., an important Wall Street executive, whose blood pressure shot up to 240 when the market went sour. Medication gave him little relief. His physician tried hypnosis. Within a week, Mr. M's pressure dropped to 175. He then was taught self-hypnosis, now possesses the means to control his own blood pressure and defeat the dangers that go with hypertension.

You can calm down almost any case of jitters with self-hypnosis. Relaxing completely, making yourself receptive to suggestion, tell your inmost mind that you have calm and firm control over your tension; you are losing your tension; it is going . . . going . . . you are no longer tense, within or without. Plant a posthypnotic suggestion that when you come out of hypnosis you will quietly handle whatever situation must be handled, confident in your ability to see it through.

A student called Dr. Caprio by long-distance and explained he had been referred by someone else. He explained he was about to report for an oral examination he needed as a requirement for his Master's degree. He was all tensed-up with panicky questions: "What if I make a bad showing?" "What if my mind goes blank when they ask me questions about my thesis?" He had not slept for several nights. Now he had no time for anything but a phone call. Could he be helped?

Dr. Caprio explained the technique of self-hypnosis and suggested that the student first analyze himself as to *why* he was afraid to face his "oral." Was he fully prepared? Had he studied enough? Was he afraid of one particular examiner? If he was sure he deserved to pass, he should go on to giving himself positive suggestions of confidence, continuing even as he approached the examination room.

He reported later that it wasn't half as bad as he had anticipated, and he was proud of his own control of the situation. He passed his examination, and now he knows how to control any unreasonable fear.

It is not always necessary—or possible—to go aside into a quiet, shadowed room when you wish to practice self-hypnosis. As you become adept, you will find that with the use of key phrases and your own conditioned receptivity, you can calm your tensions almost at once. It is as though you kept a reservoir of calm, strong confidence in your subconscious and are able to draw upon this reservoir at will.

What you should know about "nervous fatigue"

Normal fatigue is a protective device, signalling the need to rest. But there is a kind of chronic or exaggerated tiredness which comes from various states of tension, such as disappointment or anger.

Self-hypnosis can give you a flood of energy when you need it. It is better, however, to direct your self-hypnotic suggestions at the root-cause of the chronic fatigue which can drain away so much of your success and happiness. Use self-therapeutic suggestions such as these:

I am going to start every day with the wide-awake feeling that it's wonderful to be alive, facing the day's great adventure.

I am going to meet my problems with a zest to make the best of them, and see them as a chance to improve my life.

I am going to work a reasonable number of hours, relax as I work, and know I have energy to spare if I ever must work extra hours.

I am going to get around outside my job and outside my every-day surroundings, stimulate myself with interesting things to do and the company of interesting people.

I am not going to let myself enjoy spells of the "blues" or other negative emotions. I hereby declare that my normal condition is one of happiness.

I am going to be tolerant and kind in my dealings with others, avoid conflict, radiate love.

I am going to develop a sense of humor, especially the ability to laugh *at myself* when I get all tensed-up and cross and tired.

It will pay you, too, to examine the effect of your decisions upon your general states of tension and your susceptibility to fatigue. *Worry* is a prime cause of tension and tiredness. George Hawkes, a former Dean of Columbia College, Columbia University, wrote:

"Half the worry in the world is caused by people who try to make a decision before they have sufficient knowledge on which to base a decision. If a man will devote his time to securing all the facts related to his problem, his worries usually will evaporate in the light of knowledge."

If it is your habit to make half-baked decisions, and suffer the consequences, break that habit with self-hypnosis.

Before leaving this section, we should remark that a good deal of pain can be relieved or prevented by self-hypnosis. This accounts for the growing popularity of hypnosis in the dental chair.

When you need dental work, talk quietly with your dentist and ask if he plans to give you pain or discomfort. Any treatment involving drilling will suffice! Ask for a few moments alone in the chair, in which you can relax and give yourself calm, strong, subconscious suggestions so that you will scarcely be aware of the buzzing drill. It helps to suggest that you will feel completely detached from the proceedings, as though you were sitting on the roof of a building across the street and watching a stranger in the chair. This technique has worked wonders, especially for patients who have bad aftereffects from a "shot" of Novocain but now find that in many cases they can do without it.

Self-hypnosis can help you stay young and live longer

Q: What's all this fuss about growing old? Don't we all have to grow old, die and make room for the next generation?

A: *The fuss is not about growing old but about feeling and acting old long before you have to.*

A pioneer psychoanalyst, Dr. Wilhelm Stekel, searched for the reason why some men of 30 feel as though they were 60, and some men of 60 feel like men of 30. He concluded that the key factor is an emotional one. Those who seem never to grow old keep their hearts everlastingly able to respond to all that is beautiful in this world.

Medical science has established that a deficiency of hormones and other secretions of the endocrine glands has a great deal to do with the aging of the body. Side by side with this discovery has come the recognition that emotions have a great deal to do with the functioning of the glands. Thus, mind and body are not separate entities. All of us know the depressing effect of a quarrel, or of a bad-news telegram. All of us know the glowing tonic effect of good news, of a victory won, of a job well completed.

Self-hypnosis can help you turn the tide of your emotions and strengthen every emotion that helps you feel better, feel younger, live longer.

Henry and his wife made extensive preparations to spend their retirement in Florida. Then the wife died. Henry, shocked to his soul, seemed to die emotionally. Nothing interested him. He looked and acted 20 years older than his calendar years.

At last he allowed himself to be taught the techniques of self-hypnosis. Beginning with relaxation and self-analysis, he began to dispel his emotions of self-pity. He came to terms with the truth that his former source of happiness could not be regained. Gradually he began to find interest in doing odd jobs for his friends, in helping children with their school work, in vocational guidance along the lines of his own engineering profession. He began to read books he never had gotten around to reading. Best of all, he found himself able to look at the paintings which had been his wife's lifetime hobby, and instead of feeling devastated, he found the paintings a source of inspiration.

Continuing with self-hypnosis and self-analysis, he learned to live alone, to make new friends, to enjoy life, to see beauty. He made an intelligent and healthful adjustment, and now feels and looks like the man his wife knew.

Posthypnotic suggestions to remember:

I am going to keep my zest for life; in fact, I never really lost it.

I know a man is as old as he feels, and I feel hopeful, zestful, energetic.

I am not going to sit around and wait for the world to find me. I am going to do something about finding new pleasures, new interests, new friends.

Everything that amused me when I was younger still amuses me. I am going to smile more, let myself go and really laugh.

My goal is not merely a longer life, but a longer, richer life.

I am going to use all my long experience in life to build a truly interesting life.

I shall be kind, gracious and understanding, drawing the love of others old and young.

I shall keep on learning, thereby making sure that I grow wiser as I grow older.

I shall avoid self-pity, show my love of life and share it.

Use self-hypnosis to help you win all the limitless benefits of self-hypnosis

Whatever your age, whatever you want out of life, whatever may your situation, you can find vast new happiness and success by helping yourself with self-hypnosis. At the same time, suggest to your subconscious mind that you definitely shall continue with self-hypnosis—knowing it is a golden key to continued emotional maturity and lasting peace of mind.

Psycho-Emotive Reminders:

All your life you have been using mild self-hypnotism without knowing it. Now you can use this mighty prosperity method exactly as you wish, to give you exactly the results you want.

First you perfect your technique, which consists of four steps: Autorelaxation, Autosuggestion, Autoanalysis, and Autotherapy. Each of these stages provides you with important new values. The final step, Autotherapy, perfects the subconscious influences you wish to set deeply into your mind as your guides to more prosperous living.

If weight control is your problem, self-hypnosis can do it no matter how many other methods have failed. You follow a healthful routine, avoid all temptation to backslide as you progress toward better appearance and better health.

Self-hypnosis can be used almost anywhere at almost any moment. You can rely upon it for instant relief from much nervous tension, fatigue and pain. It lifts you quickly out of mental depression onto your preferred strong and cheerful level of confidence.

Self-hypnosis helps you stay young and live longer. Posthypnotic suggestions help you live a richer, fuller, more active life no matter what your calendar age may be. The self-hypnosis technique in itself can be used to help you continue and improve your own amazing self-therapy.

My Personal Notes on Lesson Three:

Suggestions:

This Lesson contains a built-in exercise in the application of situations in any Lesson to any other. Starting with the first Lesson, take each story which appealed to you and notice if it contains any elements of self-hypnosis. You may wish to do this with all the stories in all the Lessons.

There is no reason why you should not use self-hypnosis in business situations. This Lesson, however, was keyed mainly to basic *character* and *personality*. If you first apply self-hypnotic techniques in these areas, it will serve to remind you that living consists of more than making a living.

You may wish to experiment with various objects which slightly tire your eyes in looking at them, so that your eyes will close in signaling your suggestibility. The following have proved useful: a lighted candle, a gleaming ring or similar object, a whirling disk on which a spiral pattern has been painted or drawn, a pendulum which the eyes follow. You may find your own favorite object.

Record any story, "Q & A" or Personal X-ray which you seemed to "take personally."

The next Lesson reveals a few simple actions which are so psychologically loaded they release enormous new power the moment you touch them. If you're not satisfied with your current set-up, these simple actions will break things wide open—change everything for you—*fast!*

PROSPERITY QUOTIENT ANALYSIS

The following brief quiz is designed to perform two important functions:

1. Test the way you have taken in the ideas contained in the first third of the Parker Prosperity Program.
2. Emphasize and, in some cases, re-emphasize certain key ideas and psycho-emotive motifs.

Instructions:

Each of the following questions is to be answered *Yes* or *No*. Answer without reference to the book. Don't try to guess the answer, and do not change any answer after you have checked it in the space provided. If you cheat on this quiz, you cheat yourself. Remember, this is *your* book and *your* private record.

Not all items have question-marks. "Yes" or "No" therefore will indicate whether you agree or disagree with the statement given. (This is a device to help you think more accurately and to change your thinking patterns.) Use a dictionary to look up any words you may not understand.

Scoring instructions are given at the end of the quiz. Your score will reveal a significant *Prosperity Quotient*—which will improve constantly as you proceed through the Parker Prosperity Program.

Yes No

1. Do the famous *Acres of Diamonds* lectures extol the virtues of being poor? — —
2. The only reason for getting rich is to be able to do good for others. — —
3. If you ever go broke, should you resign yourself to being broke thereafter? — —
4. A public relations director working with thousands of employees found their greatest need was kindness. — —
5. When you observe that you are motivated by certain principles, can you assume the same principles motivate others? — —
6. It is not wise to list the good things you want out

Yes No

of life, for you then will be the more disappointed
if you don't get them. — —

7. Compared to lucre, we may eliminate other consid-
erations as mere bagatelles in a compendious defini-
tion of *prosperity*. — —

8. According to the Vacuum Law of Prosperity, you
should get rid of possessions you don't want—but
this applies only to material possessions. — —

9. The Law of Radiation and Attraction may be fairly
stated as: "You have to give before you can get." — —

10. When you command your good to appear, you bring
mighty forces to your aid. — —

11. You can imagine everything you desire—except
money. — —

12. When you keep company with self-confident people, do you help to build your own self-confidence? — —

13. Is it right to pray for money? — —

14. Prayers will not do you any good unless you pray in
church. — —

15. To use the prosperity law of self-confidence, you
have to be born with a lot of self-confidence. — —

16. Are you ever likely to use self-hypnosis without
knowing it? — —

17. Do you definitely know the difference between
PMA and NMA? — —

18. Is it advisable to act as old as you think you should
act, according to your age in years? — —

19. Are you facing each day as a new, great adventure? — —

20. Do you grant favors as freely as you ask them? — —

21. Do you cherish any habit which you know is offensive to others? — —

22. Do you hold your tongue when you are angry? — —

23. It's quite true, isn't it, that you cannot get tenants
for an office building when all the office buildings
around it are nearly empty—no matter what you
do? — —

Yes No

24. Is it your duty to others to point out their faults all the time? — —

25. It is obvious, isn't it, that you should borrow your attitudes toward life from others, and never attempt to build your own? — —

26. Is ordinary *hope* a prime ingredient of a positive mental attitude? — —

27. Enjoying life and participating in life helps you stay young. — —

28. It is impossible to help your health without medicine or medical treatment. — —

29. Have you keyed your goals to definite needs and lacks in your present condition of life? — —

30. Once you have gone through Benjamin Franklin's motivation method, you never should repeat it. — —

31. "We are just as happy as we make up our minds to be." Any truth in that statement? — —

32. Whether you are rich or poor, you have nothing to do with it—it is the judgment of God. — —

33. The power of human motivation was not known in Benjamin Franklin's time. — —

34. Can you transfer your own PMA to someone else? — —

35. Can PMA help anyone sell insurance to people who have had several bad years of business conditions? — —

36. Say anything you like to other people. It has no effect upon your own success. — —

37. No "hard-headed businessman" can be helped by prayer. — —

38. Don't go out and find new interests—sit around and wait for the world to pay attention to you. — —

39. Is self-hypnosis a form of voluntary psychic healing? — —

40. Forgiveness is a great help in getting rid of harmful emotional states. — —

41. Should you plan your life more than a few days ahead? — —

Yes No

42. An attitude of love is a help in successful human relations. — —
43. Do people generally like to hear the word *you?* — —
44. Is it valid to compare an individual's personality to a magnet? — —
45. Is it good to give yourself a time limit, or deadline, within which you will perform some stated achievement? — —
46. The desire for self-preservation is a valid human motive. — —
47. Should negative attitudes such as fear and hate ever be allowed to have any part in your life? — —
48. In attempting to persuade, it is best to speak in a whisper. — —
49. Look back on victories you have won, and you will see they were based on problems you have solved. — —
50. When you maintain a feeling of richness in your "mental atmosphere," is it possible for others to feel it? — —

How to rate your answers:

The following questions should have been answered *No:*
1, 2, 3, 6 , 7, 8, 11, 14, 15, 18, 21, 23, 24, 25, 28, 30, 32, 33, 36, 37, 38, 48
All others—*Yes.*

For each wrong answer, subtract two points from a total of 100. (If you did not answer, count it wrong.) For example, if you had 30 wrong answers, your score would be 40. ($30 \times 2 = 60$. $100 - 60 = 40$)

Once you have calculated your score, by all means go back to the text and check each wrong answer. It is important to have the right answer in mind before you proceed to the second third of the Program. Meanwhile:

Enter your prosperity quotient in the space below

My Prosperity Quotient on (date) —— was ——

This Prosperity Quotient, of course, is private and personal. Nobody's Prosperity Quotient stays the same—unless it happens to be perfect. After the second third of the Parker Prosperity Program is completed, you take another quiz and watch your Quotient rise.

Lesson Four

Ten Days to a Prosperous New Life

Five Simple Actions That Change Your Whole Existence—Almost Overnight

NINE MEN OUT OF TEN WHO ASK William E. Edwards for advice are worried about one thing—money.

Some are worried because they cannot meet their current bills. Some are troubled because they have let their wives down. Many say dismally that they'll never be able to afford the kind of life they want—the glamorous life of country club, fine home, Thunderbird, first-class cruises, Brooks Brothers suits.

The worries all boil down to one thing—money. They have come to the right man, for Mr. Edwards knows what it is to be pinched for money. For years he went through the dreary struggle of trying to make ends meet. Well educated, with a respectable I. Q.,

Mr. Edwards was versed in the success secrets of such great thinkers as Ralph Waldo Emerson as well as the battle-tested methods of modern captains of finance. He knew that what he missed was the way to *apply* these money-making ideas. Yet even his thorough study of business techniques did not reveal the mighty clues he knew must exist—somewhere.

A breakthrough reveals the simple actions that bring in money

One day a rich man told Mr. Edwards about one question a man should ask every time he wants to spend money. Testing this action, Mr. Edwards found it was loaded with psychological money-making power. Investigating further, he discovered the other actions, just as simple, which key one's entire being to making money. When he had made his money, he turned to explaining and illustrating the actions to other men with money worries. In ten days, those actions can change your entire existence. They are revealed to you here, now.

Action One: To give you tremendous trust in yourself

This action is the fastest confidence-builder you can use. It goes right to the heart of this whole business of self-confidence—touches off a psychological landslide that releases self-reliance on a tremendous scale.

1. Make a special promise to yourself
2. Write down that promise
3. Carry it out for ten days

It doesn't matter too much what the promise is, so long as it takes you in the direction you want to go. But you've got to write it down, and come hell or high water you've got to keep it.

Sample promises to start you thinking

1. *To keep my desk neat and orderly*
   One talented businessman thought he was such a genius he was above keeping things in order—but, genius or not, he never could find anything on his desk, he disorganized others

and kept them waiting. This simple promise immediately beefed up his production, increased the grip on himself that is characteristic of the truly successful man.

2. *To cut out the small talk*
People of stature don't indulge in a lot of small talk. This area of "tongue control" is one of the fastest of confidence-builders and status-builders, let alone adding to your efficiency.

3. *To limit yourself to one hour's television each evening*
An up-and-coming young man said: "It's not that there's anything wrong with being entertained—it's that I was not exercising my power of judgment to choose a good program and put trivia aside." Standards are important to a man who is going places.

4. *To write down each day something new you've learned*
This keys-up your desire to learn, builds your confidence in your learning ability, gives you a rich storehouse of precious material for continual use.

5. *Stop being the know-it-all at business meetings*
This man was bright—but by playing to the grandstand he made himself a nuisance instead of an asset. He glibly supplied the answer to everything, was always horning in. He was a pain to his boss, disliked by his peers, inwardly displeased with himself. His change of approach was at first hard to enforce, but soon showed him great benefits in getting across his *good* ideas.

6. *Whenever you feel like quitting at the end of an hour's work— to go on for another hour or more*
We tend to work in one-hour shifts, breaking up our work days into too little work and too much socializing. Using energy creates energy. You can stretch any work day by working an extra hour after the usual hour is up, and win a quantum rise in your accomplishment, satisfaction and reward.

The way to a self-determined life and a self-built fortune

When you make promises to yourself, write them down and keep them, you open the road to a self-determined life. The trouble with many of us is not that we lack brains or that we lack talent. Our bugaboo is the feeling that we never will be able to bring into being the kind of life we should like to lead.

This common feeling of inadequacy too often springs from the realization that we don't have ourselves in hand. Not having mastered ourselves, we stop trying to master ourselves; we come to expect a slipshod performance even though we *know* this is not the way to make big money.

The enormous paradox that cripples your earning ability

When we lack faith in ourselves, we still seek to place our faith in something. And the thing in which many such people place their faith—without ever realizing it—is *fear*. This is the enormous paradox—to place one's faith in fear, to count on fear to get one by. When you use fear as your basic method of operation, you cripple your ability to act on your own. You lose your ability to lead a self-determining existence—even to take the actions which will bring your individual talents into their greatest strength and effectiveness.

Hints for using the dynamic promise-technique that rapidly builds your self-confidence

1. Be sure to put in writing the promise you make to yourself. This gives substance to the whole idea.
2. Promise yourself to do something that calls for resolution, but don't make it so tough you won't have a chance.
3. Don't set up goals merely for the moral exercise, important as that is, but try to kill two birds with one stone. Choose an action that gives you a practical benefit.
4. Once you have promised yourself to do something, be sure to carry it out. If you go back on your word, it makes you still less confident.

Don't fool around with this technique—it's loaded

This technique is a bombshell. Its benefits are enormous, but the dynamic psychological mechanism works both ways. Keep your promise and it builds confidence—fast. Break your promise and it makes you less confident than ever. If you're smoking 30 cigarettes a day and you think you should smoke ten—but you don't think you'll be able to stick to ten—then promise yourself to smoke 15, for a starter. When you have achieved that goal for a stated period of time, set your next goal and see to it that you make good.

Q: Is it really so important to write down my goal?

A: *It's a must. Years of experience with hundreds of men show it must not be skipped.*

**Here is the record of how one young man
made out with his ten-day promise to go
on for an hour when he wanted to quit**

1st day: It was tough—but I did it.

2nd day: It seemed harder than yesterday but I didn't give up.

3rd day: I had just finished a one-hour stint when someone dropped in and wanted to chat, but I excused myself and went on with my work.

4th day: Things went better. I didn't have to fight so hard to go on for the second hour.

5th day: Told myself this whole thing is for the birds—that it's artificial and I ought to junk it—but I kept my promise anyway (a little sullenly).

6th day: Must be getting used to it. No trouble at all to work the longer period.

7th day: My assistant said to me today: "You seem to be moving fast these days."

8th day: Surprise! I'm not only getting a lot more work done, but I'm much less tired when I go home.

9th day: Worked steadily all day, found a short break is just as refreshing as a long one. The people around me seem to be catching on.

10th day: I did it. Feel substantial inside. New ambitions are rising within me and I don't see any reason why I cannot achieve them. This thing works!

What about it? If there is nothing in your performance that you want to improve, you can stop right here. But that is not likely—so take the first great action that breaks things wide open.

Make a promise

Write it down

Keep it—and feel the indescribable stir of enormous self-confidence!

Here is your own form for making your promise to yourself and keeping an honest, private record of your accomplishment

Date . . . .

I promise myself that for the next ____ days I will____

_____

Signed . . . .

How I made out with my promise:

Kept It

Yes   No   **Remarks**

1st day . . . .
. . . .

2nd day . . . .
. . . .

3rd day . . . .
. . . .

4th day . . . .
. . . .

5th day . . . .
. . . .

6th day . . . .
. . . .

7th day . . . .
. . . .

8th day . . . .
. . . .

9th day . . . .
. . . .

10th day . . . .
. . . .

Action Two: To release your mind's enormous potential for getting ideas and insights

Did you ever pick up a pad and pencil, or sit down at your typewriter, and list all the ideas you can think of on a given subject?

This simple action primes the pump of the inner mind. It's terrific for anyone who has a problem—whether it's a girl whose problem is how to find herself a job—or a tycoon whose problem is to double the size of his corporate empire.

PERSONAL X-RAY

Find something you do the same way every day. It may be going to work by a certain route or something else just as simple.

Now write down every different way it is possible to act in that respect. Don't try to be too "practical." Let your imagination roam. Whether or not you find a better way to act, you will have stirred up your idea-power in a way that may not have seemed possible.

Why it is so important to have ideas

Each of us has a storehouse of thousands and thousands of facts and impressions in his memory. Many of these facts and impressions may seem useless—but—when your mind comes up with a great idea, it simply has taken two or more separate facts and put them together!

The following example seems obvious—till you do a double-take.

A week ago, Henry Hays learned that the 100-acre Butler farm, five miles out of town, was for sale. Six months before, he had seen an obscure notice that the township was going to surface its back-country dirt roads. He'd also heard somewhere that a large corporation was going to build a new plant in town and would hire 3,000 people. While helping a friend find a house, he had found out there was an acute housing shortage.

Henry Hays bought the Butler farm, which now would be easily accessible over the improved roads. He sold it as a real estate development to house the employees at the new industrial plant, and he made a considerable profit.

Now bear in mind that Henry Hays' mind had to choose the four significant facts from among the thousands stored in his memory before he could apply those facts to the opportunity which offered.

If you're like most other intelligent people, your mind, left to its own devices, will come up with 3 or 4 good ideas a year. But when you release your mind's enormous idea-potential you can come up with 30 or 40 ideas that will really set your life on fire.

Ten minutes a day can do the trick

For the next few days take ten minutes a day to jot down lists of ideas. Force yourself to write down a list of at least six or eight ideas on any subject that is meaningful to you. You can jot down ideas for increasing your income, or a list of new products for your company to bring out, or ideas for saving money in your household, ideas for getting a better job, or improving your present job, or a list of ideas for opening up your social life, or for keeping your wife (or husband) happy.

Don't worry about how good the ideas may seem at the start. Remember, *you make lists in order to prime the pump of your subconscious mind, to trigger off its vast potential activity, to start it flashing relationships which cannot exist until you provide the raw materials.*

> An advertising man was given the job of coming up with an idea for selling a brand-new product. He sweated out 26 headlines for an ad. The boss turned them all down. Three weeks passed in which nobody else had the right idea, either.
>
> The advertising man, discouraged, was spading his garden when the time bomb went off. The idea-in-a-million hit him like a bolt from the blue. This one idea sent his career skyrocketing. It brought in money hand over fist. But where had this sockdolager of an idea come from? From the "no good" list of ideas which nevertheless had primed the pump—lighted the fuse which eventually brought forth the explosion.

How to key your ideas to a single great purpose

Here is part of an idea list made up by a young husband who wanted to get his life into high gear:

1. I'll subscribe to high-class business magazines and keep my eye on the ball.
2. I'll have lunch with as many different people as I can, each week, to find out how other minds view the world.
3. I'll see myself as a $25,000-a-year man and I'll dress like one.
4. I'll keep my eye on the next job up the ladder, see what it needs in the man that fills it, and see what I can do toward making myself that man.

He found that Ideas #2 and #4 did the trick. But every one of the other ideas helped in reminding him of his purpose.

To add extra power to your idea lists, start an Insight Scrapbook

Here's the technique:

> When you sit down to make out an ideas list, have a newspaper or two handy, and some magazines. Clip out *one* item a day for ten days. Each item must seem significant to you—it must catch your eye and your mind. Spend two minutes thinking about it.
>
> Paste each item into a scrapbook.

Why this is one of the hottest techniques a person can use in directing his ideas and his life

This simple technique shows you where your sharpest interests and your greatest powers lie. You'll see within ten days that the items you choose all have something in common—and that something is YOU. You'll get a clearer picture of the person you are—a new confirmation of the *self* which yearns for its dynamic, liberating fulfillment.

> A man felt he was not using his capacities. He had a smallish job with a large corporation—an outfit that made big money in the financial field. When he heard about the scrapbook suggestion, he kept one side-by-side with his lists of ideas. Here is how his scrapbook looked—somewhat rearranged since these pages are not as big as scrapbook pages.

NEW YORK HERALD-
TRIBUNE, SEPT. 17

(Rides. Canadian Pacific Railway announced plans early yesterday to cut passenger fares beginning Oct. 27 in a move to halt the continuing decline in passenger revenues. Details will be announced later, the privately-owned carrier said. Next, the government-owned Canadian National Railways said it would introduce new services and cut fares by up to 58 per cent, starting Oct. 27.

NEW YORK WORLD-TELEGRAM AND SUN
SEPTEMBER 18

SONJ Head Hopeful Of Oil in North Sea

Associated Press

NEW ORLEANS, Sept. 18.— The head of the world's largest oil company believes prospects are bright for discovery of oil or gas in the North Sea.

"The North Sea really is a popular hunting ground these days," said M. J. Rathbone, board chairman of the Standard Oil Co. (New Jersey). "The area today looks like Libya about five years ago.

Rathbone made his remarks yesterday at a news conference after speaking at the final session of the annual meeting of the Independent Natural Gas Assn. of America.

He said Jersey Standard is one of about 20 companies currently conducting geophysical explorations in the North Sea.

NEW YORK HERALD-
TRIBUNE, SEPT. 19

Aussies Shuck Royal for Dollar

CANBERRA.

Australia's new decimal currency will be headed by the "dollar," Harold Holt, the Treasury Minister, announced yesterday. This reverses the June decision to use the name "Royal" for the new currency units.

Mr. Holt said the government had not selected "dollar" originally because it would not be a distinctive Australian name but there was now clearly a major body of opinion in favor of it Serious consideration had been given to "pound" but there would have been technical difficulties in introducing a new unit with the same name as the old but only half its value.

Australia hopes to introduce decimal currency by February, 1966.

NEW YORK WORLD-TELEGRAM AND SUN
SEPTEMBER 21

Natural Gas Business Sees Booming Future

Associated Press

WASHINGTON, Sept. 21.— Until and if the United States runs out of gas, no end to the growth of the natural gas business—a dramatic chapter in the nation's industrial history —appears in sight.

When oil producers started harnessing the gas that blew out of wells drilled for oil, a giant new industry was born. Some wells had been drilled mainly for gas but it wasn't until oil operations started capturing the gas from their wells, instead of letting it go to waste, that the natural gas industry really got going.

NEW YORK HERALD-TRIBUNE
SEPTEMBER 22

❡Prices. Companies were busy marking up prices and catching up with competitors who had already marked up theirs. The steel industry was caught in a price parade when Jones & Laughlin, fifth largest steel producer, lifted prices of most lines of oil country tubular goods about 4 per cent. Next came U. S. Steel, followed quickly by five other companies. In New York, lead moved up ¼ cent a point to 11¾ cents, the seventh price increase since November. One of the major textile manufacturers, Cannon Mills, Inc., announced increases of 2 per cent in terry cloth prices. Retail prices, however, will not be affected until mid-1964. *Over-all, the price boosts did not appear dangerous enough to stir fears of inflation. Economists put the movements down as the stirring of a normal economy.*

NEW YORK HERALD-TRIBUNE, SEPT. 23

PRE-CLIPPING THE PRESS. When Fortune arrives in the mails tomorrow it'll report that merchants are more optimistic about the next few months' prospects than they have been in years. For '64 auto dealers are very bullish, all home-goods merchants in this semi-annual survey look for a 6 per cent hike in volume. Clothing retailers see a 5 per cent increase. . . . Fortune's economists say builders think apartment-building will hit an annual rate of 550,000 family units this year

NEW YORK HERALD-TRIBUNE, SEPT. 24

Autos

❡Indicator? The first 1964 models in the showrooms touched off a buyer response that would gladden the heart and pocketbook of any auto maker. In this\case, Chrysler was the happy manufacturer with the initial entries in the 1964 auto market race. In two days last week, it sold 11,490 new Chryslers and Plymouths. A year earlier, the Chrysler division took 10 days to sell 19,109 new models. *The buying climate appears to be on the level of the 1955 model year, which was the greatest in the history of the industry," an executive observed with elation.*

NEW YORK HERALD-TRIBUNE, SEPTEMBER 25

The world's population explosion, unchecked and untouched by modern scientific and technological developments, is getting to be far more menacing to the survival of mankind than any other event of history.

That's the sum and substance of a massive (680 pages), analytical study prepared by the United Nations Demographic and Social Statistical Section and entitled Demographic Yearbook, 1962.

Consider, for a moment, the following facts of the population bulge:

In mid-1961 the world population was approximately 3,069 billion.

—During the decade of the '50s, the population increased by 560 million, which is greater than the total population of India.

—Since 1960 the bulge was bigger by another 61 million, or an annual increase equivalent to three times the population of Argentina or one-third that of the United States.

The UN study shows that between 1950 and 1961 the annual rate of the "explosion" was at 1.8 per cent, but during the latter part of the same period the pace quickened, reaching 2 per cent between 1960 and 1961.

There are now 23 persons for each square kilometer of land in the world, compared with 18 ten years ago.

NEW YORK WORLD-TELEGRAM AND SUN SEPTEMBER 26

Shares listed on the New York Stock Exchange have passed the 8 billion mark, the Exchange announced today.

The Exchange estimates that the 8 billion milestone was reached with the start of trading yesterday in 1,479,725 additional common shares of ACF Industries Inc., issued in a 2-for-1 split of the manufacturing company's stock.

The Big Board's list has about doubled since 1956, both in number of shares and market value. Since reaching 4 billion in March, 1956, shares listed have increased at an average rate of about one billion every two years. The latest billion was added in the 22-month period since November, 1961.

Market value—computed at $224 billion in March, 1956—passed the $400 billion point last month.

One morning this man attended an executive meeting. When the discussion got around to economics and finance, he sensed a new confidence and spoke up, quietly making a few well-founded observations on the economic picture. This was his great break-through in the company; a year later he was working in high eche-lons. Yet until he started his scrapbook he had not realized the "hook" his mind needed. He'd always read newspapers and maga-zines but until then he had not found the focus for his thinking and the springboard for ideas which "came naturally" to him for-ever after.

Of course you'll keep up your scrapbook indefinitely—and go over it from time to time. Your scrapbook will kick off a thousand ideas. Here is a diagram which shows what happens when you choose, say, ten scrapbook items from among a couple of hundred you read:

**Each tab around the frame represents
an item you skimmed—some 200 in all.**

**This diagram
shows how ten
items out of
200 caught
your eye.**

**The ten items
show where
your real
interests
lie.**

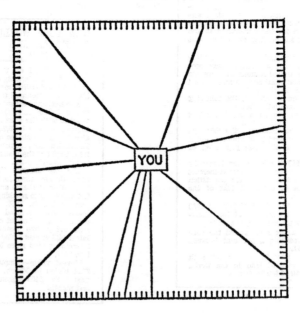

Action Three: To help you recognize and build every part of your capital

Here's the technique—with a powerful Personal X-Ray built into it:

Every time you spend any money—whether it's a nickel or an important sum—ask yourself this question:

"Will this expenditure further me in reaching my financial goal?"

Now, this is at least a triple-barreled question. You're talking about money, that very useful, measurable and indispensable commodity. But you also are reminding yourself of everything else you can and should spend with an eye toward reaching your goals—your time and your energy, to say the least.

A young man who came to Mr. Edwards for advice said that he wanted to have a quarter of a million dollars by the time he was forty. He smiled at the suggestion that he should ask himself: "Will this expenditure further me in reaching my financial goal?" every time he spent a dime for a newspaper.

Yet he did go along with it—and now enthusiastically recommends this simple and amazing way to bring yourself up sharp a dozen times a day, make yourself mentally picture your goal and *face the big question of whether you really are going after it.*

The same young man a few months later:

His progress at first seemed slow. By questioning his expenditures he'd put himself a dime ahead, a quarter ahead, a dollar and a quarter ahead in one week. Meanwhile he was being paid $5,500 a year as a management trainee, chosen because of the exceptional score he received on an aptitude test. He had no college degree, however, and the Big Boss seemed to favor men with letters after their names.

This young fellow was a nut about cars. He was offered a wonderful buy in a bucket-seat convertible with twin carbs and ground-out cylinder heads. But he asked himself the big question (above) and decided to spend the money—and three nights a week—getting his degree in Business Administration.

Now came the payoff. With two years of hard study ahead of him, he felt the strength that comes with knowing what you want, going after it, and even depriving yourself of something which did not lie on the direct road to your ambition. Filled with new decision, he went to his boss—told him he was working on his degree—reminded the boss of his high score on his aptitude test—gave him facts and figures to show how well he was doing on his present job. He was courteous—but strong.

The boss was a bit taken aback by this show of force. He knew that forceful young men were apt to leave the company if they didn't get what they wanted. So the young man was given the next good opening that came along—a good spot in the middle executive group—a strong and definite step toward a quarter of a million dollars, which started with questioning even a ten-cent expenditure.

How do you invest your time? And your energy?

Do you spend your evenings aimlessly? You can have more fun in time allotted for fun than in time frittered away.

Is at least half your reading related to your main goal?

Do you spend at least half of your lunch hours in good, successful company?

Is your hobby just a hobby—or do you allow it to muscle in on business time and business energy, even to the extent of the Monday morning charleyhorse?

Are you sure you're in the right job? If not, are you doing something about it?

Do you waste energy on emotional upsets you could avoid—often by taking the "medicine" of concentrated work?

Have you set down your goal in writing, and outlined every step leading toward your goal, so that you really know when you are wasting—or using—money, time and energy?

Action Four: To break through the barrier that limits the size of your thinking

When the great psychologist, William, James mentioned that most people use only one-tenth of their brain power, he hit it on the nose.

To break through the barrier that limits the size of your thinking—and so the size of your life—do this:

Imagine that you're suddenly faced with the necessity of doing things on ten times the scale of your present performance.

The editors of Parker Prosperity Program venture an educated guess that your reaction is:

"You're crazy!"

Fine! The whole value of this technique is the shock and the jolt it gives to your thinking. We desperately need something to shock us out of our habitual routine of small-time thinking.

Q: Doesn't the majority of the population avoid big thinking?

A: *Now you're on the trail! Most men can't see themselves doing anything bigger than, say, moving up from a Falcon to a Buick, from a $12,000 house to a $20,000 one, maybe from $8,000 a year to (whew!) $12,000. You would not be reading this Prosperity Program if you didn't want to think and be bigger than that—so take yourself right out of the majority of the population.*

Is there something sacred about $12,000 a year?

Strange how this approximate figure sets the ceiling for so many men who *could* use it as a springboard for leaping upward! Let's see how the as-if-ten-times technique took hold of a man who never had tried to paint his life on a big enough canvas.

A $12,000 department head was summoned to the president's office. He felt uneasy, but reassured himself that everything must be okay. Profits had gone up about ten percent each year he had been running the department. Arming himself with his latest Profit and Loss statement, he headed "upstairs."

The president said: "John, I see you have some good stuff in you, but your department showed a profit of only $100,000 this year."

"Yes, Mr. Wells, but that's ten percent over last year."

Mr. Wells paused, smiled. Then came the haymaker: "In the next two years I want to see your department show a profit of one million dollars."

John thought the president was joking. After all . . . a ten-times increase! But the president was not joking. What's more, he told John he could keep his present staff but he could not increase it. When he showed a million in profits his salary would be jumped to $25,000 and he'd be in line for more.

The president saw John's shock, heard his slightly dazed: "I'll try." Yet by the time John returned to his desk, he was moving in a new world. He sat down and made lists of every process, every sales method he used. Soon he saw ways to save on manufacturing costs. His product was books, and he realized he'd never tried to sell books a thousand at a time to big corporations. And why not bring out a $300 Culture Library? And what about the market for art prints, using the thousands of names of customers he already had in his files? And what about. . . .

He'd never *had* to think ten times bigger. Now he did, and communicated the feeling to his entire staff. In two years his profits were $1,180,284 and he said that was peanuts.

The as-if-ten-times technique increases every energy and capacity

Here is one of the greatest of all psychological miracles. When we envision king-sized goals, the inner self automatically finds ways to supply what it takes to reach those goals. You can use this technique in your business, you can use it in charity's work, you can use it in exerting your power and influence over others, you can use it at home, you can use it anywhere.

In a very little while, jobs that used to seem "big" don't seem worth mentioning. For a physical example: Suppose you're going to lift a five-gallon can of gasoline. You've done this before, so you set your muscles to lift the weight. (It's 35 pounds.) But this time the can is empty. You lift—and the three-pound weight goes sailing over your head. Your 35-pound tug has become automatic.

It works the same way with your mental muscles.

The great advantage of the as-if-ten-times technique is that it breaks you out of squirrel-cage thinking. Sit down right now and apply *ten-times* thinking to your business or your job.

Your "as-if" form to propel you into the ten-times technique

Date . . . .

I'm going to break through the ceiling that limits the size of my thinking. To achieve this I'm going to imagine that I must multiply by ten ....

(Fill in your goal on this line.)

Here are some of the actions I'm going to take to achieve it:

1. ....
2. ....
3. ....
4. ....
5. ....
6. ....
7. ....
8. ....

You can use this technique to skyrocket your income—to become ten times as good at your job—to become one of the world's greatest experts in any field—to become a great cook—to achieve power and prestige—to achieve anything you want, without limit.

Do not neglect to fill in these forms. You must *see* your exciting new ideas for achieving great vision and accomplishment!

Action Five: To increase your effectiveness immediately—in your present setup

Emerson said:

> "Don't waste life in doubts and fears; spend yourself on the work before you, well assured that the right performance of this hour's duties will be the best preparation for the hours or ages which follow it."

The five great Actions which propel you toward money and the enjoyment of money do not require you to stop what you are doing and to dash out on some quixotic adventure. Rather, they take hold of you as you are and your job as it is—then rapidly and vastly expand your horizons.

What is the *right* performance of this hour's duties? The performance that is so good, it immediately makes you worth more. So—here is the technique which increases your effectiveness and value immediately, on an ascending scale:

Ask yourself this question about everything you're doing: "What is the heart of this problem? This project?
This operation? What one, two or three points are the
high-performance essence of the matter?"

Here is the technique that makes you stop wasting your strength,
lets you put your energies where they exert leverage and move
your world. Here is what makes one person a pigmy and another
a giant.

The boss who got lost with a slide rule

A fussbudgety old-timer was enmeshed in the details of working
out a new floor plan for his department. Suddenly he was presented
with an opportunity where huge profits could be made by fast
action. Instead of seizing his big break, he went on with his slide
rule, figuring where file cabinets and wastebaskets should be
placed. He came up with a fine floor plan—and lost half a million
dollars.

"As you wander on through life, brother, whatever be your goal . . .

. . . keep your eye upon the doughnut, and not upon the hole."
The saying is too ancient to get a credit line, and it is common
sense in letters ten feet high. When have you acted like the hide-
bound old-timer? How often have you confused effort with achievement—put down a *small* hook for a *big* fish and wondered why it
got away?

List half a dozen successful company presidents and see how they use this rule

Of course they do! One company president took less than a
minute to jot down for us a list which is worth study both for
what it includes and *what it leaves out:*

1. Constantly getting new products and constantly improving
   the old ones
2. Marketing those products dynamically
3. Keeping costs down
4. Keeping everyone stirred up and planning ahead

This man won't discuss a minor problem with anyone. He says that people will solve their own minor problems if you don't do it for them and in most cases it won't make any difference whether they solve them or not.

Success is where you make it—and this technique makes it everywhere

A man was promoted to Scout executive in a big suburban county in which scouting was just limping along. The facilities were there, the boys were there, even the woods were there; but not much happened.

> This man was an exponent of "the thing that matters." He saw that the success of scouting depended on his ability to get enough good men to act as Scoutmasters. This was the pivot on which everything hung. He focused all his energies upon it. Once he got 30 good men to volunteer their services, everything else fell into line and scouting boomed in that county.

You can see what is important when you get the habit of looking

This technique develops in you a sharp sense of the relative importance of things. It also helps you look closely at people and give them what is important to *them*—an indispensable aid in getting results.

> One man had friction with his wife. He tried to butter her up by bringing home expensive presents. Eventually he let her run up as big a telephone bill as she wanted—saved a lot of money and achieved harmony in his home.

> A real estate man kept his REAL ESTATE sign freshly painted and his office comfortable and well-equipped. He knew his business, yet he wasn't bringing in the customers. He realized that other real estate offices in town were better located, yet he could not get space in a desirable location. Observing that people always are interested in making money, but put an inward defense against spending it, he changed his sign to REAL ESTATE INVEST-MENT CENTER. He followed through on the theme in his advertising, trained his salesmen to talk *investment*, and the world beat a path to his door.

Don't worry about oversimplification

Some people object that this technique will lead them to over-look some angle that matters. Actually it works the other way. This technique sharpens your entire perspective in business, domestic matters, social matters . . . every side of your life. And even if you do miss out on some point that looked small but wasn't, you'll never be so badly off as though you were fussing about every little thing and losing the all-important sense of directed drive and concentrated focus.

You can use this technique any time and everywhere. Try it for ten days. Try reducing things to their few *essentials*. See how it immediately increases your capacity. See how it launches you off to the kind of life you want—starting from where you stand right now.

Here is a small form for the *few* things that matter:

The problem ....

Here are the few things that matter:

1. ....

   ....

2. ....

   ....

3. ....

   ....

4. ....

   ....

Get started—get living!

We have seen these actions show a salesman his strong point and multiply his selling power by ten.

We have seen them make a woman a regular powerhouse in getting the kind of home she'd always wanted, that her small-thinking friends scoffed she'd never get.

We have seen these actions give a man such self-belief, make him so strong and attractive in character that he easily dominated those around him.

We have seen these actions enable a person to come to a decision in three minutes on a situation he'd thought he never could cope with.

We have seen these actions invigorate a man who was dead broke and skyrocket his income past $100,000 a year.

The line-up is endless—but the actions are quick and few. You perform them in minutes and the power they release goes rolling on and on. Remember that these actions bring material success—but that's not all they bring. They give you the true basis of inner self-esteem. They give you everything you need for every part of prosperity.

Psycho-Emotive Reminders:

All the ambition in the world will not put money into your pocket if you do not release and strengthen the dynamics of your personal drive. These five actions get you going almost overnight:

Make a promise to yourself and keep it strictly. Whether it's a promise to keep your desk neat or to limit television time or whatever it may be, it becomes a self-renewing energy-cell of confidence, casts out fear that you can't get what you want.

Release your mind's enormous potential for getting ideas and insights. Make lists of six or seven new ideas on any subject meaningful to you. Fill your mind with ideas so that new relationships—the key to great idea breakthroughs—are continually encouraged to flash through. Also start an Insight Scrapbook to reveal the point where your key interest lies.

You have money capital, energy capital, time capital. By the simple action of making sure that every expenditure of money is relevant to your goal, you take hold of the complete idea of capital, automatically increase your store and channel it toward your ambition.

Insist on the necessity of doing things on ten times the scale of your present performance. This is one of the greatest of all psychological miracles. It not only makes you know you can reach your greatly enhanced goal, but also provides the means and the energy you need for getting there.

Starting where you stand now, make sure you concentrate on the few important points which stand at the heart of any task or problem. When you put your energies where they have most leverage, you can move your world.

My Personal Notes on Lesson Four:

Suggestions:

Pick up the statements of *goal* you have written as directed in previous parts of this Program. Examine them again and especially go over the steps by which you aim to achieve your goals. See if they really are the important steps.

Observe men or women who are adept in moving into new situations or new jobs and quickly taking control. Notice how they make use of all or most of the five key actions set forth in this lesson.

Record any story, "Q & A" or Personal X-ray which had special meaning when you read it. Keep up the practise of adding little tabs to the book at those pages, for your future easy reference.

The next lesson is an eye-opening treatment of the fine art of swaying opinion and action. It gives you the universal tool of Emotional Appeal, enables you to use this sound and dramatic device in selling anything, in getting your way with others, in building your success through a high level of personal power.

The Magic Prosperity Power of Emotional Appeal

How To Cause Others To Think, Act and Speak in Ways That Help You

YOU CAN GET OTHERS TO WANT TO listen to your spoken words and read your written words.

When people *want* to pay attention to what you say they are easily swayed, commanded. They are happy to do what you want them to do. And you can wield this priceless power through the straightforward techniques of Emotional Appeal—the method that gets YOUR way with an uncooperative mate, stubborn child, stonewall customer, unfriendly neighbor, difficult boss . . . even when reasoning or demanding won't work!

101

Begin by remembering the following critical statement about *preoccupation*. This is a key statement which Roy Garn has taught to thousands of pupils in his Emotional Appeal Institute in New York City. This statement backs up Mr. Garn's entire course, the essence of which you receive in this Lesson.

Here is the critical statement:

**Preoccupation prevents your reaching
and commanding the minds of others—
and everybody is preoccupied**

Q: I see great merit in my preoccupation with my business and personal affairs. What's wrong with preoccupation?

A: *Nothing is wrong. In fact, preoccupation is quite necessary and natural. But you still have to break through the other fellow's preoccupation before you can make his desires less important than yours.*

Words are emotional pranksters. After they leave our mouths, they step aside to see what happens. And what happens always happens to somebody. That somebody is our Listener. Either he remains preoccupied because our words lack a stimulating Emotional Appeal, or the Emotional Appeal is so powerful that the Listener changes his mind even though he hadn't wanted to!

At a Las Vegas gambling house, a staid Philadelphian lost a hundred dollars, one dollar at a time. Being down to his last twenty dollars, he changed it into silver dollars and put fifteen of them into an inside pocket so that he would not put them on the dice table. Now he once more approached the table, holding only the five dollars which represented all he'd allow himself to risk. But the knowing lady *croupier* sized him up and said: "Move over, folks! Here comes a real player!" The Philadelphian's two hands hit the table at the same time, betting his entire twenty dollars. He lost it—to an Emotional Appeal.

A man who had a weak heart had to remove a pile of discarded builder's sand from behind his garage. But the day of the willing—and low-paid—handyman seems to have vanished, and he could find nobody to do the job for three dollars, four dollars or even five dollars. Watching some boys expend a great deal of energy in their play, he offered to pay one dollar to the boy who shoveled the most sand after he said the word GO. He got his sand shoveled with no further persuasion, and the boys even brought their own shovels.

Ability to use Emotional Appeal to sway others can be extended indefinitely, used in innumerable situations, pile benefit upon benefit until it represents the greatest power you possess.

Emotional Appeal at your command improves not only your power to persuade but also your outlook, your personality, your job and personal relationships, the success of your marriage, even your physical health. As you will see before you finish this Lesson, Emotional Appeal can be used to improve yourself just as surely and strongly as you use it to win the attention and cooperation of other people.

Here is a graphic view of the basic setup for using Emotional Appeal:

Notice there are just four main Emotional Appeals. These are all you need in order to cover everything you say or do in changing refusal into acceptance, disinterest into friendliness, NO into YES a thousand times over.

Remember them as the Fatal Four and let us see exactly how they help you get what you want out of life.

How to use SELF PRESERVATION as an emotional appeal

You're a sweet old lady.

(Chances are you are not; but didn't that announcement snap you out of any preoccupation which may have crept in?)

You're a sweet old lady and you board a bus to take you into a strange neighborhood. Timidly you ask the bus driver to let you off at Pine Street. He snaps back that he has enough to do with making change and watching traffic, so he'll remember to stop at Pine Street—maybe! "Ah, you'll remember or you might get killed!" says the sweet old lady in gentle alarm. And having penetrated heavy layers of grim preoccupation, she adds: "There's such a dangerous excavation at that corner!" He remembers!—although somehow the excavation does not appear.

You're a housewife. Your self-preservation naturally extends to an interest in anything which will lessen the work and fatigue connected with cooking meals, cleaning house, riding herd on children, let alone trying to look pretty for Hubby when he comes home. Preoccupied, you skim the pages of a magazine, barely glancing at three or four ads for flour—until one ad stops you. JUST ADD WATER, it says, because everything else is *in* to make perfect pie crust. You buy!

You're a prosperous businessman with money in your pocket, driving on a lonely street in a tough neighborhood. As you stop for a red light, a character opens your car's door, holds a knife to your ribs and says, "Gimme your wallet." Without turning your head, you say: *"I'm on duty* and I can't take my eyes off that green car stopped a block ahead, so beat it." He beats it.

PERSONAL X-RAY

Write down half a dozen situations in your life in which you are not making headway. Look for the SELF PRESERVATION angle that can give you the breakthrough you need. First read the *helps* which follow the form.

Situations	*Angles*
1.	1. . . . .
	. . . .
2.	2. . . . .
	. . . .
3.	3. . . . .
	. . . .

Situations	Angles
4.	4. ....
	....
5.	5. ....
	....

HERE ARE SOME HELPS IN SPOTTING AND USING POWERFUL ANGLES OF *SELF PRESERVATION:*

Look for an appeal to *HEALTH*

An old man wanted to sell the farmhouse which had sheltered four generations of his family—and had not been "kept up" lately. He put a bargain price on it, but no sale. Finally he announced to all comers: "This place is only for folks who'll live to be a hundred!" This preoccupation-breaker of course brought the interested question: "Why?" The old man then pointed to the open porch which faced southwest and announced that that porch got more square feet of sunshine per day than any other place in the state. He sold the house.

Look for an appeal to *RELIEF FROM A NUISANCE*

Doctor D. could not get Patient E. to reduce; but if E. didn't lose 30 pounds he'd be in trouble. At last Doctor D. explained that if E. didn't object to carrying 30 pounds of extra weight, he shouldn't object to having a small sample case containing 30 pounds of stones chained to his wrist. E. agreed, thinking it a big joke, but soon found it such a nuisance to carry around 30 pounds of stones that he took off 30 pounds of flesh and got rid of the sample case.

Look for an appeal to *PRESERVATION OF A LOVED ONE*

This closely corresponds to self-preservation, especially when a child is involved. A man who sold a book on child-rearing tried to sell it by radio, but found that mothers were so preoccupied with their household duties that his commercial fell on too many unheeding ears. He solved his problem when he began by saying loudly: "Did you ever feel like rocking your baby to sleep with a baseball bat?"

Look for an appeal to PROTECTION OF PROPERTY

The owner of a parking lot saw business and traffic move out of his neighborhood. Other parking lots were filled while his was half-empty. He changed his sign to PROTECTED PARKING (the protection had been there all the time) and filled his lot every day.

Now go back to the form on Page 104 and fill it in carefully. This Prosperity Program gains lifetime wealth-producing value as you consistently change it from a general Program to a Program that means *you*.

HOW TO USE THE MAGIC OF *MONEY* AS AN EMOTIONAL APPEAL

Have you ever seen this ad in your daily paper?

The Reason Why

The reason why I have hitherto been able to sell my goods so much cheaper than anyone else is that I am a bachelor. I do not need to make a profit for the maintenance of a wife and children.

It is now my duty to inform you that this advantage will shortly be withdrawn. I am about to be married.

I therefore urge you to save money and make your purchases at once at the old rate.

O. Kayser

It's a safe bet you have not, since this ad is over 100 years old. Many a slick adman of today could "improve" it with various gimmicks. He hardly could improve on its results, nor on its basic appeal of MONEY.

Everybody wants money and the security it seems to promise, and we usually try to make (and keep) money with as little expenditure of self-preservation effort as possible. One of the deepest fears is to find one's self without money or to have to part with it unexpectedly; or, with some people, to part with it at all. That is why *MONEY!* is one of the greatest preoccupation-breakers you can use.

Apply emotional appeal to your own attitudes toward money

First of all, it's only money! If you let it become all you are pre-occupied about, you'll collect it, all right. Then what? Let one horrible example provide the answer:

> An elderly man was taken into court, charged with being a book-maker. Else, how could he account for having $16,800 in his mis-erable bachelor quarters, on his salary of $56 a week? He was dis-charged, with the court's wry apology, when he proved his means of saving so much money. He'd never taken a girl on a date, never drank or smoked, lived mostly on buckwheat he bought in whole-sale lots, wore a beard to spare the expense of shaving, had charged 12% interest on a 15-cent loan to his grandmother . . . and allowed himself a movie three times a year, provided he could get in for no more than fifty cents!

Note these two truths about gaining a true consciousness of money and how it comes and goes—and if these statements con-flict with some more generally-accepted ideas, remember this: We are concerned only with attitudes which help you *make* big money so that you can *spend* big money.

1. Money values and attitudes are better learned by *spending* than by *saving*.

   Hold onto the principle, and you'll see that the practise is not as drastic as it may seem. You can save a good deal of money by cutting your consumption of small items which do not have much emotional meaning to you. You are then in a better posi-tion to buy the big items which really do buck you up and by their very existence in your life provide a boost and a drive toward making more money. You can first search the emotional content of a large purchase, perhaps asking advice, and see what it really means to you.

2. "Living on a budget" is good only if you enjoy it.

Budget "living" is meaningless unless you can adjust your emotional needs to your budget's limitations and objectives. Otherwise, see yourself as a person who does not so much need the RECOGNITION factor of Emotional Appeal—we come to this later—as he needs more freedom with which to spend his money, perhaps in ways that make more money.

Turn Item Two into a Personal X-Ray. Sit down with yourself and find out if you are a person who can intensify your drive for achievement with a budget that keeps you toeing the mark— or a person who is better off in his own self-created atmosphere of inflowing and outflowing money. Then—be yourself!

The many-sided appeal of money

The police department of a small town could not get motorists to drive slowly when their sign said SPEED LIMIT 30. They got the results they wanted when they changed the sign to 30 MILES OR $20. The appeal is to the *fear of loss of money*.

Las Vegas, Monaco, and similar havens of gambling glitter on and on with their promise of *easy money without work*. How often does it happen?

Stocks and other securities are routinely sold by pointing out the significance of your money in providing "grow power" to industry, and so forth. It seems almost wicked not to *let your money work for you*.

Advertising's favorite words and phrases are such as *Free, Bargain, Sale, Two for the Price of One,* and so forth. Here you are *preserving your money*.

The most practised method of earning big money may not do very well for you unless you pause to think now and then about money itself; most of all, about the powerful emotional aura that surrounds money. Some of the biggest money-makers of all history had this instinctive grasp of money's meaning. Anyone can find it and use it for Emotional Appeal with a thousand angles of profit.

And if you ever want to hold the attention of any number of preoccupied people, wave a fistful of money in front of them! Or

drop a handful of change and see how many dozens of preoccupied heads turn toward that inviting jangle.

HOW TO USE *ROMANCE* AS EMOTIONAL APPEAL IN SWAYING OTHERS

Let us pause to recognize that people are not set up in black-
and-white emotional patterns. There is quite a lot of overlap. Yet
almost any person can be *typed* as to the major Emotional Appeal
which will do a job on him.

Q: How can you tell?

A: *Observe; it's plain as day. Be definite in your observation.
Limit categories to the Fatal Four—self-preservation, money, romance, and recognition. Almost anybody will put aside his preoccupation for any of these Appeals; but each has his major leverage-
Appeal. Watch him in action awhile and you'll see it.*

Any girl, plain or pretty, can get a husband

Attracting a husband has little to do with a girl's face, figure,
age or financial status! When she meets an available man she wants,
the right Emotional Appeal will bring a proposal.

> Jim and Grace planned a party to announce their engagement.
> Grace's mother said half in jest: "There won't be another pretty
> and unmarried girl at that party! I'll see to that!"
> And so, in a modest but becoming dress, we see Barbara, Grace's
> "noncompetitive" cousin. She was quite plain, a bit older than Grace.
> And a bit wiser. She wanted Jim, and she knew the Appeal that
> best levered him.
> Grace had been boasting that her marriage to Jim would be a
> 50-50 partnership. Barbara said that when *she* was married, her
> husband would be the boss and especially would hold the purse-
> strings. In other ways she told Jim that when *she* was married,
> she'd take the role of a dedicated helper to her husband . . . she'd
> feed his ego as well as his waistline . . . and again she mentioned
> MONEY.
> Jim married Barbara, and it was best all around. But it wouldn't

have happened if Barbara had not observed Jim awhile and seen the kind of wife he really wanted.

By itself, Romance as an Emotional Appeal consists of: sexual attraction and the desire for marriage; the future promise; the new experience.

Sex fulfillment and satisfaction are part of Self-Preservation; sex *attraction* and *desire* make up the highly-charged content of Romance.

Romance also lends itself especially well to combinations with others of the Fatal Four Emotional Appeals. Here is a combination that works beautifully with the kind of man who is prone to take a girl out on a date, escort her to her door, say good-night and forget her.

Let the wise girl not say: "Thank you for a lovely evening." This has too much *finality*.

Let her say instead, in the dark, on her doorstep: "Do *all* your lady friends have such a lovely evening when they're with you?"

Watch him smile, glow, blush a bit, then sputter. You have rocked your gentleman friend with the power of RECOGNITION! Whether he then boasts, denies or says you're kidding—or just looks wise— he likes it! When at length he goes home, he's far more likely to come back for more of that warm glow he gets from you.

Women respond too! A specialty shoppe had trouble in moving their more lacy and revealing nightgowns until the more modest gowns were labeled FOR SAINTS while the go-go gowns were labeled FOR SINNERS. This also resulted in a number of double sales, when girls bought one of each so that the salesperson would not know if they were a saint or a sinner.

Promise is a mighty part of ROMANCE

You'll recall the cosmetics manufacturer who implied a promise of beauty and made a fortune. The *implication* of promise was sufficient. He gave each customer HOPE.

When an undergarment, perfume or reducing method implies a promise to make us appear more attractive (Romance), and when in addition it may sing in strong undertones of Self-Preservation

(You can be beautiful and healthy, too!)—sales are made in billions of dollars. Entire industries are supported. Fortunes are built.

"Romance can't do much for *my* product," growled a builder of earthmoving machinery, gesturing at his 20-ton, scarred and muddy product with its double row of six-inch steel buckteeth.

But in his advertising he *promises,* even if the promise is merely: "Lasts Longer."

And that is why anyone in any business constantly should refresh himself with the amazing power of Romance Emotional Appeal—because it depends so much on PROMISE.

Whether in love, health, money, appearance, satisfaction, recognition or in any other way, we all strive towards some form of perfection. We tend to pay attention to anyone whose words and actions help us move mentally in the direction of the perfection we want. The world moves on emotional appeal because the world is made of people—and people want to fulfill themselves, and will fill the pockets of anyone who shows them how.

Using recognition appeal to achieve personal success

Tell a person he's important. Tell a manufacturer that his product is important. Show a person how to make himself or his product or his services or his child important. This is the essence of Recognition Appeal, and it sways people individually, by groups, and by entire nations. As the fourth but not least of the Fatal Four, it wraps up a vast deal of personal influence you may not sway with the other Appeals; also, it blends very well with any of the others.

> Some decades ago, the program of the Metropolitan Opera House was a flimsy, one-sheet affair, so poorly printed that it smudged the white gloves of opera-goers. Today it is an attractive small magazine on slick paper, supporting itself well on advertisements. But the man who first said he'd put ads into that program almost went broke before he used Recognition. He said: "You know what an exclusive organization the Metropolitan Opera is—so only the most outstanding companies are being invited to advertise. This is your opportunity to be included—or be left out!"

> A milkman regularly left milk in a metal-lined box at the home of

a middle-aged widow. One day he cut his finger on a jagged piece of metal protruding inside the box. He left a note for the lady of the house—"Please fix your box"—but she never got around to it. After cutting himself again, he left a bigger note. She expressed sympathy, promised she'd get it fixed, but still didn't get it done. When he cut himself a third time, he left a note which said: "I am your milk box. Please fix me. Everything else is so pretty inside and outside your house, I feel as though I don't belong." The box was fixed.

In human communication, the Emotional Appeal of Recognition can instantly break preoccupation, enter a mind or change a mind. It relates to pride, opinion, appreciation, identification with clothing, appearance, behavior, events, people—and just about everything else.

It is also the great prime mover in just simply getting along with people and making them like you. Anyone who is interested in becoming prosperous knows how important that is!

To make people your friends, show them you are IMPRESSED by their words, actions or possessions

It's as simple as that!

It's also amazingly all-pervasive. Every conversation with anybody becomes a chance to show that person you recognize his importance—and so add power to any influence you may wish to have upon him, because he tends to trust you and like you.

Conversation secrets of recognition appeal

Read with a pencil in your hand. When you come to a technique you habitually use, put a *plus* next to it. When you come to a technique you should be using but neglect to use, put a *minus* next to it.

1. Use your ears

Teach yourself to *listen* when others speak to you. They may not be saying very much, but show them *they break your preoccupation*. At the same time, listen for clues which reveal the direction of *their* big preoccupation-breaking Emotional Appeals.

2. Listen with your eyes, too

Your depth of interest is mirrored in your eyes and your surrounding expression. This much-desired bit of Recognition always will serve you—and you need not say a word. Practise this *attentive silence* which makes such an emotionally-satisfying contact between listener and speaker.

3. On most occasions, remove your worries, operations, children, finances and complaints from your communications with others.

If you are asked about these, keep your answers smiling, courteous and brief—not emphasized at the expense of the other fellow's interests. Dwell upon such matters and you let the other fellow wander back into preoccupation.

4. Don't hammer-in any superiority you have, or think you have

When you do this, you belittle your listeners. Two men were running for Congress. They spoke from the same platform. One, who had been a general in World War II, pointed out that he had been in that position of great responsibility while his opponent had been nothing but a private. Then his opponent rose and said: "All those among you who were generals, vote for him. All those who were privates—vote for me!" The ex-private and his Recognition Appeal won the election by a huge margin.

5. Keep most apologies out of your conversation

Why? They draw attention to you! If you are unavoidably late in meeting someone, let the extent of your apology be: "Sorry I inconvenienced *you*. I know I'm late." Ending it there leaves the other fellow retaining the advantage. The same applies to over-elaborate remarks you may wish to make about your un-combed hair or unshined shoes. Or for a child's childlike performance at the piano.

6. Pay a compliment if you can, or at least show the other person's existence means something to you

A student in one of Roy Garn's classes was a traveling salesman. One of his problems was in getting a good haircut from a strange barber. When he used Recognition he usually got the right haircut. Before sitting in the barber's chair, he would smile and nod to the barber, and invariably received a smile and a nod in return. Shortly after the barber began snipping, the salesman would say: "You have such light hands, I hardly can feel I'm getting a haircut." He found that barbers approached in this way often gave him so much time and attention, they kept their regular customers waiting.

Then there is perhaps the great compliment-story of all time, a perfectly true one. Clarence Darrow, the famous attorney, told a friend that his will provided for cremation of his body, the ashes to be strewn from a hill overlooking Jackson Park in Chicago. The friend sighed: "If such an event comes about, a man will have to walk all over Jackson Park to get a decent legal opinion!"

To win Recognition you must give Recognition

People who desperately want recognition are likely to overdo their use of that big little word "I." To be more listenable, likeable and persuasive—and, in the end, get more Recognition—use pronouns with Recognition Appeal. Use words like *you, we, us.* Say it's OUR problem, YOUR family and mine.

If you want people to do jobs for you, give them some form of Recognition. Where attendance at meetings of a civic organization had fallen off, it picked up suddenly when the reception committee for a prominent speaker appointed a large number of vice chairmen.

By understanding the impressive importance of Recognition, you can identify it quickly in yourself and in others, and make better use of it. The main point is this: *Be sure to tell the other fellow somehow that he is important; but, no matter how important you think YOU are, let somebody else tell YOU.*

You can command a situation merely by asking questions—as long as you pack your questions with Emotional Appeal

Have you ever noticed the many activating advantages offered by questions? They are inherently preoccupation-breaking. Consider:

"Nice day, isn't it?"

"Is this the second floor?"

"May I have the address where you wish to have it sent?"

"Do YOU like getting pushed?"

Questions put the other person on the defensive. They can change an attacker into a defender. They can be used to confuse, to delay, to get information the other person would rather not give—as any cross-examining attorney can tell you.

> One of Mr. Garn's female students was held up by a man with a gun who demanded her money and her jewelry. Taking her time to unclasp her necklace, she remained calm and prodded him with questions. "Is this the only way you earn your money?" "Isn't it dangerous to keep a gun in your pocket?" "Have the police ever caught you?" "Is that the same kind of gun that cowboys use?" Trying to hasten the robbery and answer questions at the same time, the holdup man became confused. "Damn you, lady, you've got me all mixed up," he muttered, and backed away without taking anything.

Her questions had emotionally upset his offensive. This is an unusual case, of course, but you may use the same technique with anybody who heckles you.

Notice too that questions allow your listener to speak—you give him recognition—yet also sustain interest in *your* subject! And furthermore, questions bring objections out into the open and can give you valuable insight into what's really on the other fellow's mind.

Pack your questions with emotional appeal

1. Word your question to encourage the answer you want

   To a young mother: "Wouldn't it be wonderful if you could have more time for relaxation?" (Or maybe—". . . . to help your children with their studies?")

   To a mail-order executive: "How would you like to become the biggest man in the mail-order business?"

   In short, you are saying: "Of course you'd like to take a big step nearer to the perfection you want!"

2. Be sure your audience knows the answer

To a trout fisherman: "Do you have a favorite bait for trout?" It's a great Emotional Appeal to get a man talking on his hobby!

To an executive: "Which qualities do you believe are most important to make a man successful?" Ditto for any man's area of competence!

3. Use leading questions wherever possible

These are so effective, they are not allowed in cross-examinations during trials! For example—and notice the double impact of your words:

"You want a man who knows your local problems, don't you?"

4. Objectively relate your question to the situation, the time and the listener

"How would you like to keep weeds, bugs and insects out of your garden forever?" This is a sales-compelling question which includes most of the Rules for Asking Questions. It is extremely effective when used on transient customers in the garden department of a house furnishings store. Were you to ask it in the hat department, say, it would fall flat on its face.

Let's see how a slight switcheroo tied in beautifully with Romance appeal. When the proprietor of a photography studio sees unmarried girls "shopping" for prices on portrait photographs, he asks: "Do you know why we're called the *lucky photographers?*" When the girls answer *No,* he produces a handful of bridal photographs and remarks: "These girls posed for us less than a year before they were married." The girls not only forgot price and bought portraits; they recommended the photographer to their friends!

5. Have an emotional Fatal Four relationship between your question and the listener

"Would you like to have more pep?" (Self-Preservation)

"Want to make $100 quickly, easily and legally?" (Money)

"Doesn't it get you peeved when you pay $35 for a radio that your friend buys for $20?" (Money and Recognition)

6. Use a "choice" question when you want definite action

"Will you contribute one dollar, or would you rather contribute more?"

"Isn't it wiser to protect our children now—than to see them crippled later?"

"Do you want insurance today or a lawsuit tomorrow?"

Q: But the calm lady who confused the holdup man with questions didn't use any emotional appeal.

A: *This is a subtle and important point. The situation was so loaded with emotion that her matter-of-fact questions brought in an opposing atmosphere which simply did not belong with a gun and a threat. It was emotional conflict that got the gunman confused!*

Prepare yourself for prosperity by relaxing— with inward-directed emotional appeal

Surely you have noticed that people who live successfully are masters of a certain basic relaxation. They don't panic, they can take one thing at a time, their abilities are not crippled by tension, they sleep well.

To relax successfully, you must successfully communicate with yourself, break your own preoccupation, and control the Emotional Appeals which most strongly activate you.

You are ready to do that right now. Knowing the Fatal Four Emotional Appeals, you can identify your own motivating Appeals. Many other Lessons of this Prosperity Program will be of help in doing this.

Identify your major Emotional Appeal and your second most important one.

Concentrate your attention on any aspects of the *other two* Emotional Appeals. For example, if Recognition and Romance most rapidly awaken response in you, concentrate on the remaining two—Money and Self-Preservation.

For Money, imagine finding money or a valuable object such as a diamond, or winning a big prize or gaining a reward. For Self-Preservation, you might imagine eating a food you enjoy, doing a disliked chore with new ease and enjoyment because you have found out a new method, sleeping in a hammock under swaying palm trees, cleverly getting out of some dangerous situation—and so forth.

Now you have broken your preoccupation with your two major Emotional Appeals! You'll find, with practise, that you can do this whenever you wish. And then—here's the magic!—the two Emotional Appeals on which you have concentrated also will leave your mind because they are not naturally your preoccupation-holding interest!

A student said: "I never realized how relaxing it is to be able to clear my mind completely. Didn't realize, either, how much tension you build up when you *can't* clear your mind."

Use the Emotional Appeal Technique for Relaxation at least ten minutes a day. To summon sleep, use it before retiring. Use it before a conference. Use it before trying to unravel a problem. It has an amazing power to renew your energy, to relax you into confidence and optimism, to put you in touch with your best self and clear the road that leads straight to prosperity.

Psycho-Emotive Reminders:

Emotional Appeal techniques make people want to listen to you and makes them believe in you. You can get your way with an uncooperative mate, stubborn child, stone-wall customer, difficult boss—even when reasoning or demanding won't work.

Preoccupation prevents your reaching the minds of others—and everyone is preoccupied. Emotional Appeal helps you break through this preoccupation and make your desires more important than the other person's. You also can reap vast benefits for yourself.

The Fatal Four Emotional Appeals begin with Self-Preservation. This includes health, getting rid of threats, preserving loved ones from danger, and other techniques. When you write down half a dozen situations in your life in which you are not making headway, you can see where a Self Preservation Appeal can give you the breakthrough you want.

Money is a powerful Emotional Appeal. You see that spending rather than saving, and *not* living on a budget, may be your clues to making big money. Alerted to the power of Money Appeal, you can see dozens of ways in which to sway others in the particular situations which occur in your life.

Romance Emotional Appeal builds entire industries and makes fortunes. You see how it gives both men and women great personal power—how its major ingredient, *promise*, carries over into all forms of influence and persuasion.

The Emotional Appeal of Recognition helps you wield influence and control even in casual conversation, adds vast power to any form of selling. Through the Emotional techniques of asking questions you control situations and make them go the way you want them to go.

Emotional Appeal can clear your mind of distracting thoughts, help you relax and sleep better, feel better, use all the tremendous energies and talents that wait inside your mind.

My Personal Notes on Lesson Five:

Suggestions:

Observe three or more persons who generally seem to get others to go along with them, yet are well-liked and respected. Watch for the Emotional Appeals they use.

Ask your librarian for a collection of great speeches. Read some old speeches and some modern ones. Make a checklist of Emotional Appeals:

Self-Preservation	Romance
Money	Recognition

and check each one as it occurs in these speeches.

Record any story, "Q & A" or Personal X-ray which had personal meaning when you read it. Many readers find it pays to write out these items separately and make a special reference book. In addition, do not neglect to mark them in this book as a further reminder.

When items do not remind you of yourself, but do remind you strongly of someone you know, jot his initials next to any such item.

The next lesson picks up many hints we have dropped concerning the power of your subconscious mind. A Man of God shows you that within your subconscious you can find a scientific law which decides which prayers are answered and which are not! This law can work miracles in your life . . . miracles of prosperity and abundance . . . miracles of healing, happiness and love.

How to Mine the "Mother Lode" of Your Subconscious Mind

The Key to the Most Awesome Mental Treasure Within the Reach of Man

A GRIZZLED PROSPECTOR LEADS HIS burro through a range of dry and barren hills. At last he finds a shallow stream. Patiently he scoops up water and sand, swirls it in a pan, watches—and after many tries, sees the glint of gold! After many days or weeks, he may fill a tiny sack with pinhead-sized nuggets.

Yet he knows this trickle of gold washed down from *somewhere*. Upstream he seeks for the great vein of gold which will make his fortune. Years later, perhaps, someone finds his bones, remains of hands still outstretched and seeking the one great Source . . . the *Mother Lode*.

121

Thus may we go through life gathering occasional small bits of prosperity, while the great Mother Lode of a life's fulfillment seems ever to retreat beyond the next hill, around the next corner . . . or was it back there somewhere, one inch below our unheeding feet?

Your treasure always is with you in your subconscious mind

We have used the term *subconscious mind* quite often. It is well known—as a couple of words—but few know its true significance. Fewer still know how to use its power. Dr. Joseph Murphy, Director of the Divine Science Movement and a counselor of vast experience, has explained both the *meaning* and the *use* of the subconscious mind in a way which has led thousands to prosperity. This lesson is built upon Dr. Murphy's methods.

This lesson is a special exercise in subconscious choice

In this lesson you may make many check-marks—or none at all. Probably you will make at least a dozen, and they will be of the utmost significance. We shall come back to this point. Meanwhile, check or underline any word, phrase, sentence or paragraph which particularly touches you. While we have made liberal use of lists and other guidance devices, you will not find such aids in this chapter. Attempt to let your deepest *self* guide your hand.

Caruso and the "Little Me"

Caruso, the great operatic tenor, once was struck with stage fright. His throat was paralyzed by intense fear which constricted the muscles. In a moment he had to go out upon the stage—but how could he? He said: "They will laugh at me. My career is ended!"

Suddenly he shouted at those who surrounded him behind the stage: "The Little Me wants to strangle the Big Me within!" He said to the Little Me: "Get out of here! The Big Me is now ready to sing!" When the call came, he walked out upon the stage and sang gloriously and majestically, enthralling the audience.

There is the secret! Caruso's "Little Me" was the bundle of fears, doubts, roadblocks, trip-ups which seem to dwell somewhere within every human nature—*but can do us only the harm we allow them to do.* Caruso's "Big Me" was his constructive subconscious power.

As with Caruso, so with you can subconscious power speak authoritatively to any self-imposed limitations, saying: "Get out! Begone! I summon my true strength and I rise to the summit of my chosen achievement!"

Your subconscious mind accepts
what is impressed upon it

Psychologists point out that when thoughts penetrate to your subconscious mind, impressions are made in the brain cells. As soon as your subconscious accepts any idea, in particular an idea of *purpose,* it uses every bit of knowledge you have gathered in your lifetime to bring about that purpose.

Your subconscious, however, is not the reasoning part of your mind. That function belongs to the conscious, the "everyday" section through which you make your conscious choices; for instance, the books you read, the jobs you take, the food you order in a restaurant. Within your conscious mind you are conscious of pros and cons . . . you may argue a point before coming to a decision. Your subconscious, however, is like the soil which accepts any seed, good or bad, and then proceeds to grow what has been planted. Negative, destructive points of view will work through the conscious mind to ensure that you have negative, destructive experiences. Constructive, prosperity-oriented points of view grow into prosperity just as surely as an acorn grows—not into poison ivy!— but into an oak.

Suppose you are seeking the answer to a problem. Your subconscious will respond, searching your entire life's experience for the answer, and will feed the ingredients of the solution to your conscious mind for action. That is, it will perform this seeming miracle if you have so conditioned it! If you believe: "I'm all mixed up—there's no way out, no answer," you absolutely cripple the constructive power of your subconscious and all it will tell you is the bad news you subconsciously want to hear. But when you KNOW with cheerful confidence that your subconscious WILL guide you to an answer, then it is as though the gears of your mind all mesh together and you think with a brilliant directness that gets the wanted results.

Practical techniques for mental healing through the subconscious power of prayer

So powerful is the subconscious mind that when it is conclusively focused through complete belief, it can have remarkable healing effects upon the body. Prayer is an ideal focusing agent.

Dr. Murphy suffered from a malignancy of the skin. Medical therapy had failed to check the growth, and it was getting progressively worse. A clergyman explained to him the inner meaning of a sentence in the 139th Psalm: "In thy book all my members were written, which in continuance were fashioned, when as yet there was none of them." He explained that the term *book* means the subconscious mind which can fashion and mould the cells of the body.

Tapping his watch, the clergyman said: "The watchmaker first had to have an idea in mind before the watch became an objective reality. Likewise if the watch is out of order, the watchmaker forms a firm idea of how to fix it before he fixes it." He went on to say that the subconscious intelligence of the body knows exactly how to heal, restore and direct all the body's vital functions, but we ourselves must give the subconscious the perfect idea of health. This would act as cause, and the effect would be a healing.

Dr. Murphy now prayed in complete faith, acknowledging the infinite intelligence which reflects itself in our subconscious minds. Obliterating negative images, he gave life-giving patterns of wholeness, health and perfection to his subconscious mind. Two or three times a day he went aside and repeated his affirmation. In about three months his skin was whole and perfect.

How prayer can release the kinetic energy of the subconscious mind

A psychologist was told he had tuberculosis in one lung. At night as he drifted off to sleep he quietly affirmed: "Every cell, nerve, tissue and muscle of my lungs is now being made whole, pure and

perfect. My entire body is being restored to health and harmony."
After a month, the X-Ray revealed no further lesions.

He explained that the kinetic action of the subconscious mind is very strong during the sleep period. Hence, it always pays to give the subconscious something good to work on as you drop off into slumber.

All authenticated cases of healing through subconscious power —and they are many—reveal one common quality: The ailment never is mentioned. It is never mentioned even in ordinary conversation. The only sap from which ailments draw life is your attention to them, your fear of them. It is actually possible to become your own mental surgeon by focusing, through prayer or quiet affirmation, the amazing energies of the subconscious mind. Just as we firmly image life's goals of high earnings and other forms of prosperity, so must we firmly image the essential life goal of health—and thus draw upon mighty health resources which each of us bears in the inmost part of his being.

How to remind your subconscious of your right to be rich

Money should mean to you not merely the freedom from want, but beauty, abundance, luxury, all kinds of freedom. When money circulates freely in your life you are economically healthy. Your subconscious feels this, and despite temporary setbacks—which never can "throw" you—proceeds to direct the conscious mind toward actions which make you healthier still.

Why many people do not have sufficient money

As you read the Parker Prosperity Program, no doubt you often say to yourself: *I am worthy of a far higher income than the one I receive*. Of course you are! Most people do not earn one-quarter of what they are worth. Moreover, what stands between most people and the wealth they deserve is not the excuses they may make or the circumstances they may blame, but their failure to inform their subconscious minds that they *completely expect* to earn a good sum of money.

Silently or openly, too many of us condemn money. We refer to it as "filthy lucre." We say that "money isn't everything"—which is very true—but we allow this attitude to repel money. Many have a sneaky subconscious feeling there is some virtue in poverty. "I am broke, but I don't like money. It is the root of all evil," says a bitter man, thereby displaying a considerable neurosis. Your subconscious mind can help you earn millions and still have inward peace, harmony, continued personal growth.

Don't sign the blank checks of poverty

You sign blank checks when you make such statements as "There is not enough to go around," "I will lose the house because I can't meet my mortgage payments," and so forth. Your subconscious mind takes your negative statement as your *request* for lacks and limitations. Your subconscious never rejects *anything* you drill into it.

You and your subconscious speak the same language

The language in which you think is a vast tool for building— or a vast wrecking bar for tearing down. You do not have to explain "wealth" to your subconscious; if your language is English, it knows what you mean.

Find quiet times during every day to repeat softly and prayerfully to yourself: "Wealth . . . success." Note there is no conflict in these words. You are not saying to yourself, "I am wealthy" if it happens to be untrue. But the *feeling* of wealth in the subconscious produces wealth to satisfy the feeling!

It is as though your subconscious mind were a most remarkable bank which dependably paid you several hundred per cent on every dollar you deposited. Deposit the deep conviction of *wealth* and your deposit is continually magnified. Meanwhile, of course, your conscious mind makes definite plans leading toward definite goals. It is as though your conscious mind provided a pattern which your awakened subconscious fills in.

Is it right to pray for money?

The question is asked to startle you. Anyone who doubts that it is right is filled with self-doubts that hamper him at every turn.

You have a limitless power of prayer. Repeatedly we have seen prayer's power to soothe, to strengthen, to harmonize the mental and physical manifestations of the being. Yet it goes far beyond this!

There is always a direct response from the Infinite Intelligence of your subconscious mind to your conscious thinking and your conscious action—which now is *guided* as never before. Only remember that if you are to receive, you must ask out of the quiet depths of a profound subconscious *believing*. Then your mind moves from the thought to the being. Unless there is first a firm image in your mind, it cannot move, for it would have no direction. You must reach a point of true acceptance in your mind; an unqualified and undisputed state of agreement.

This contemplation should be accompanied by a feeling of joy and restfulness in foreseeing the certain accomplishment of your desire. (Of course *money* is only one possible desire. You can and should pray for health, love, success, anything good and worthy.) It is a wonderful experience to feel your conscious mind gain a definite response from your subconscious with its boundless wisdom and infinite power.

When you pray this way, your prayers are answered. They may not be answered immediately. They may be answered in some way which at first you may not realize is the answer. But they are answered. And after awhile, as experience gives you boundless faith, you live amid all the prosperity of your answered prayers . . . all the harmony of a mind which has found all its own divine greatness.

Your subconscious mind can free you of fear

This Lesson began with an incident in the life of Enrico Caruso. Few of us ever will step upon the operatic stage, but the essence of the story is universal. Fear is man's greatest enemy. Fear grins evilly behind almost all failure, illness, debility, conflict, unhappiness. Yet fear is nothing but a thought in your own mind. Sometimes we may be afraid with good reason, as in some situation which threatens life. Most often we are afraid of nothing but the fearful *thought,* which another thought can banish!

A young medical student was the most brilliant person in his class. Nevertheless he failed to answer simple questions in written and oral examinations. It developed that he spent several days before the examination in fearing that he would not pass it. Thus he requested his subconscious mind to see to it that he failed, and of course he did.

He learned that his subconscious mind kept a perfect record of all he had learned during his medical training. Every night and every morning he began to imagine his mother congratulating him on his wonderful record. As he began to live with the happy result, he called forth a reciprocal response from his subconscious. Imagining the desired end, he willed the means to the realization of the end. He became relaxed, peaceful, confident. He passed his next examination with flying colors, and had no trouble thereafter.

This too is a story with universal implications. We have to "pass exams" in many business and personal situations which call upon us to show all of our strength, wisdom and serenity. When a fear-thought enters your mind, move mentally to its opposite of courage and confidence. Place your attention on the result immediately desired. With practice you can get absorbed and engrossed in your desire, knowing that the subjective viewpoint is what really moves you.

Fear of water, high places, closed places and similar conditions of "threat"

We have a powerful instinct of self-preservation. Because of this, some threat to life may linger as a continued fear long after the threat itself has been overcome. Here the real fear has moved itself into the region of fancied fear. Again let the mighty subconscious mind "talk turkey" to its own instincts and prove the point that *any* fear-thought can be overcome.

A boy of ten, who could not swim, fell into a pool. He nearly drowned before he was rescued. For the next 30 years, he feared the water. Then a psychologist urged him to go down to the pool when he could be alone and say: "I am going to master you. It is natural and easy to swim. Water buoys up the human body when the body is relaxed, so I am going to be relaxed and confident as I go into the water. I am going to master you. I am going to have fun swimming in you." After awhile the man *knew* this was so. He then took lessons and in a little while was swimming with no fear and great enjoyment.

The familiarity technique of overcoming fear

Many people have a fear of traveling by airplane. Here is a technique which banishes the fear and can be used to banish many other fears: *Become familiar with the situation and your subconscious accepts it.*

Spend a little time each day at an airport. Watch the huge, powerful planes come and go. Think of the investment made in these multi-million-dollar machines on the strength of their reliability. Read the timetables. See how casual and businesslike they are. Imagine 100 people seated in a plane, reading magazines, chatting, accepting food from the stewardess, and getting to Chicago, say, because the plane simply starts for Chicago and gets there. If you talk with an airline's publicity man, he can arrange for you to sit awhile in a grounded plane and get the "feel" of it. Climb in and out a few times. Also give yourself mind-pictures of the beauty of the earth as you see it from a plane, the clouds, the horizon.

One woman who had been terribly afraid of heights, and therefore of air travel, said that suddenly she became eager to accompany her husband on a flight and hardly could wait for the plane to take off! Thus it is when the subconscious makes its mighty breaks through the walls of false fear. And when you conquer one fear, it becomes easier to conquer every other.

Your subconscious mind as your partner in success

Three steps lead to genuine success. As you read them, notice how closely they are connected with all we have said about the subconscious.

The first step is to find out the thing you love to do, then do it. The man in a job he doesn't like is badly hampered. The man in a job he enjoys may feel he really is not "working," yet achieve tremendous accomplishments and rewards. When you love your work, you are all the more encouraged to find out more and more about it, keep up with latest developments. Moreover, others feel your interest in your work, and trust you accordingly. Loving your work is the largest part of success.

The second step is to specialize in some particular branch of your work and know more about it than anyone else. A young man who at first was content to be a "chemist" tripled his income after he specialized in a branch of chemistry, plastics, which he saw was keyed to modern conditions. A local real estate broker became known as an expert in finding industrial sites, and soon found himself sought out by companies in a dozen states. The world wants experts.

The third step completes the circuit of work, reward and happiness. You must be sure that your job does not redound to your success alone. Your work must benefit humanity. Confidently know that you are blessing and serving the world, and a great cup of blessings will return to you; a cup that runneth over.

The morality of true success is an important subconscious morality

Someone may object: "But Mr. X made a fortune in selling fraudulent oil stock." Money obtained by fraud often takes wings and flies away; or, if it stays, it brings trouble. When we steal from another, we steal from ourselves. The subconscious mood is not one of real success but of guilt, a form of fear. Without peace of mind there may be money, but there can be no success, no prosperity in its full and beautiful sense.

> A man in London amassed a considerable sum of money. He lived in royal fashion, had a summer home in France. Happy? He was miserable, because he had been an extremely "successful" pickpocket. He suffered from many inward disorders associated with his sense of unworthiness. Although he was not wanted by the police, he surrendered himself to Scotland Yard and served a prison sentence. After his release he sought counsel, discovered honest prayer and at length found happiness in helping others.

How to become successful in buying and selling

In buying and selling, as in all your other affairs, think of your conscious mind as the starter, of your subconscious as the motor. You must start the motor before it can perform its work.

The first step in conveying your clarified desire or image to the deeper mind is to relax, immobilize the attention, be truly quiet. This relaxed and peaceful attitude prevents false ideas from interfering with your mental absorption of your ideal.

The second step is to begin to build the reality of that which you desire. For example, you may wish to buy a home. In your relaxed state of mind you will affirm in your own words: "The infinite intelligence of my subconscious mind is all-wise. It reveals to me now the ideal home which is in a lovely environment, meets with all my requirements, and is commensurate with my income. I request that I shall find this home, and I turn over the request to my subconscious mind because I know it responds to the nature of my request. I release this request with absolute faith and confidence and I wait confidently for the answer as a farmer waits confidently for a good seed, sown in good ground, to grow."

While this affirmation has not been stated as a prayer, many will prefer to form it into a quiet prayer. The answer to your prayer may come through your seeing an advertisement, through the cooperation of a friend, or through your own keen notice of a home which is exactly what you are seeking. Let it only be reasonable to suppose that the home exists, and your subconscious mind opens every possible avenue that can lead you to it.

Perhaps you wish to sell a home

Affirm slowly, quietly and feelingly: "Infinite intelligence attracts to me the buyer for this home who wants it and prospers in it. This buyer may look at many other homes, but mine is the only one he wants and will buy, because it is precisely right for him and our infinite intelligences reach toward each other. The buyer is right, the time is right, the price is right. The deep currents of my subconscious mind now operate to bring all together in divine order."

Always we come back to the mighty power inherent in visualizing WHAT YOU WANT so clearly and unmistakably that all your inner forces and even forces beyond yourself go to work to help you get it.

A famous oil magnate said that the secret of his success was his ability to see a project in its completion. He closed his eyes, imagined a huge oil refining complex with its "farm" of huge tanks, network of pipes, tall fractionating towers, trains running here and there, and so forth. Having seen and felt the pre-fulfillment of his prayer, his subconscious mind brought about its fulfillment in reality.

When you imagine an objective clearly and forcefully and in perfect faith, you will be provided with the necessities, in ways you know not of, through the miraculous power of your subconscious mind.

Why grow old?

Your subconscious never grows old. It is part of all that is timeless, ageless and endless.

A group of eminent medical men at the De Courcy Clinic, in Cincinnati, Ohio, reported that years alone are not responsible for bringing about degenerative disorders. These same physicians stated it is the *fear* of time, not time itself, which has a harmful aging effect on our minds and bodies.

"We do not count a man's years till he has nothing else to count"

Thus the poet and philosopher, Emerson, reminds us that your character, the quality of your mind, your faith and your convictions are not subject to decay.

Along with these, the strength and tone of your glands, your muscles, your entire body can continue in good condition when you feel in your subconscious mind that your outlook continues to be young, your spirit continues to be vital.

Job said: "The thing which I greatly feared is come upon me." Many people fear old age because they *anticipate* mental and physical deterioration as the years advance.

What kept a man like George Bernard Shaw active and fully creative when he was past 90?

Why did Alfred Tennyson write one of his most famous poems when he was 83?

How could a man like Socrates learn to play musical instruments for the first time when he was 80?

Who would think that Michelangelo painted some of his greatest canvases when he was past 80?

Even today, when the average life-span grows longer and longer, it is not medicine that keeps people in their 80's and 90's going strong. (Medicine might be able to keep them *alive,* but there's more than merely staying alive to real *living!*)

Speak to any wide-awake senior citizen and you can feel the spirit that dwells deeply within his subconscious mind . . . the spirit of faith, enjoyment of life, participation in life's goodness.

Expect to succeed and you help yourself mightily to succeed.

Expect to stay young and you help yourself mightily not to grow old—save in unimportant outward appearance.

Your subconscious mind never sleeps, needs no rest. Let it know how you wish to be guided—then trust this mighty hidden power to guide you! You have found the Mother Lode of lifetime treasure because, of course, you never lost it! Now recognize it—and the gold of a good life is yours.

At this point, go back and refresh yourself on the phrases or sections you checked. Then turn to the Psycho-Emotive Reminders on the next page and see how closely your own choice of important points agrees with the Reminders. They need not agree. In fact, any differences will point up the very important matter that this Prosperity Program must reflect itself through *you.*

Psycho-Emotive Reminders:

Within you dwells power you can reflect into outward experience and lifelong success. Caruso called this inward self the "Big Me," as contrasted to the "Little Me" which is weak and fearful. Whether your outward self reflects the Big Me or the Little Me depends on the convictions you carry in your subconscious mind.

Your subconscious does not reason; it accepts. But once it accepts, it works through the conscious mind to give you the kind of life you subconsciously desire. Your subconscious can be focused by firm faith and prayer even to summon the healing forces of your body and cure "uncurable" conditions.

You can remind your subconscious of your right to be rich or of your desire to be poor, and it will deliver. Break the habit of thinking that money is unworthy or that poverty has any virtue. It is good to pray for money, and you may focus your subconscious forces best through the power of prayer.

With simple techniques you can sweep away your fears of people, of circumstances, of physical conditions. You can excel where you used to fail, free yourself of any self-made chains of doubt.

In buying and selling as in other forms of business, your subconscious can set up conditions which lead to success. When you subconsciously picture what you want, fully and beautifully, your subconscious finds the means of fulfillment.

Your subconscious never grows old. Fear of old age has much to do with premature aging. Long past threescore and ten years we can achieve and enjoy, once our subconscious minds glow with inward faith and energy.

My Personal Notes on Lesson Six:

Suggestions:

Observe some person who has a tendency to be ill. See if you discover a subconscious wish to be ill. (He may show in words and action that he accepts his self-image as a sick person)

Speak to your family doctor about the effect of the subconscious mind upon the health. Most physicians have a great store of true stories on this subject.

Talk with a person who tries hard but gets nowhere and see if he has a firm inward image of where he wants to go. Then talk with a person who has arrived, and see if he always knew where he was going.

Already you have recorded sections of special meaning to you. It is as well to go back in a few days and see if other sentences or paragraphs ask for your attention—and underlining.

The next lesson reveals a startling discovery made by a plastic surgeon. He shows you how your own "emotional surgery" removes invisible-but-real scars and defects and brings a sparkling personality, wealth, social success and happiness within your reach!

PROSPERITY QUOTIENT ANALYSIS

As with the first Prosperity Quotient Analysis, this Analysis at the two-thirds mark of the Parker Prosperity Program is designed to:

1. Test the way you have taken in the ideas contained in the Program so far.
2. Emphasize, and in some cases re-emphasize certain key ideas and psycho-emotive motifs.

Instructions:

Each of the following questions is to be answered *Yes* or *No*. Answer without reference to the book. Don't try to guess the answer, and do not change any answer. If you cheat on this quiz, you cheat yourself. Remember, this is *your* book and *your* private record.

Not all items have question marks. Your "Yes" or "No" therefore will indicate whether you agree or disagree with the statement given. (This is a device to help you think more accurately and to adjust your thinking patterns.) Use a dictionary to look up any words you may not understand.

Scoring instructions are given at the end of the quiz. Your score will reveal a significant *Prosperity Quotient*. Undoubtedly it will be higher than it was before, and will continue to increase as you proceed through the Parker Prosperity Program. If it is lower, however, don't be concerned. This only means that the prosperity techniques are still taking hold in your mind. In a little while they will become completely effective.

                                                Yes No

1. Your fears and doubts can harm you, but only if you let them.   — —
2. Does your subconscious mind ever communicate with your conscious mind?   — —
3. To increase your self-trust, make a promise to yourself and do not keep it.   — —
4. Is it true that many men use *fear* as their basic method of operation?   — —

Yes No

5. The Fatal Four emotional appeals are Self-Preservation, Money, Romance, and Recognition   — —

6. The best kind of apology is a long, elaborate apology.   — —

7. You cannot be hypnotized against your will.   — —

8. Emotional appeal will never help a plain girl win a husband.   — —

9. Self-hypnosis can free you of the need to rest no matter how hard you work.   — —

10. Most people earn less than they are worth.   — —

11. A guilty conscience can prevent you from enjoying the money you made wrongly.   — —

12. Is it relaxing to clear your mind completely?   — —

13. For best results, keep all emotion out of any questions you ask.   — —

14. PMA will cause you to attempt success only where others have succeeded.   — —

15. "The right performance of this hour's duties" conquers many doubts and fears.   — —

16. To know what is important, get the habit of *looking* for what is important.   — —

17. Can you test your suggestibility in self-hypnosis without the help of anyone else?   — —

18. Money, energy and time are the three kinds of capital.   — —

19. You cannot relieve your own discomfort in a dentist's chair.   — —

20. What you say is important to your prosperity— but not what you think.   — —

21. Does it pay to keep reminding yourself of your major purpose?   — —

22. Don't wait for other people to tell you how important you are. *You* tell *them*.   — —

23. When you ask the right questions you can take control of a situation.   — —

24. The Fatal Four emotional appeals work only in the atomic age.

Yes No

25. When a man wants to become prosperous, can his standards of entertainment make any difference? — —
26. Quit work the moment you feel like quitting. Is this a prosperity habit? — —
27. The more you believe that money is the root of all evil, the more money you'll make. — —
28. The "familiarity technique" is of great value in overcoming illogical fears. — —
29. You should identify your two major emotional appeals—then concentrate on the other two. — —
30. Is it better to allow time for fun, rather than fritter away your non-working time? — —
31. Great stage performers never need help from their subconscious minds. — —
32. Only a madman thinks he can increase his achievement by a factor of ten. — —
33. Can you attract happiness? — —
34. When you DO IT NOW, you reinforce your prosperity habits. — —
35. Should you be concerned about helping strangers? — —
36. Your instinct of self-preservation is stronger than any possible hypnosis. — —
37. New discovery in weight control! Use self-hypnosis and ignore calories! — —
38. The key words for quick self-hypnosis are secrets known only to a chosen few. — —
39. Can you decide for yourself what you want self-hypnosis to do for you? — —
40. Solicit of life that it provide a minimum subsistence and it is of ominous probability that *minimum* will become the starveling synthesis of your life. — —
41. Are goals important in helping a person rise in his job? — —
42. Each day, write down something new you learned. — —
43. There's no use in trying emotional appeal when reasoning and demanding won't work. — —

Yes No

44. To "reach" a person, first break through his pre-occupation.   — —

45. Can you fall into a habitual routine of small-time thinking that hurts your prosperity?   — —

46. Does it pay to know more about a job than anyone else knows?   — —

47. Is self-condemnation a key to prosperity?   — —

48. Emotions affect the functioning of the glands.   — —

49. Your subconscious mind accepts only ideas that are good, true and beautiful.   — —

50. Can the subconscious interpret a negative statement as a *request* for lack and limitation?   — —

Here's how to rate your answers:

The following questions should have been answered *Yes:*
1, 2, 4, 5, 7, 10, 11, 12, 15, 16, 17, 18, 21, 23, 25, 28, 29, 30, 33, 34, 35, 36, 39, 40, 41, 42, 44, 45, 46, 48, 50
All others—*No.*

Now score yourself, deducting two points for each question answered incorrectly. (Follow the rules explained in the previous Prosperity Quotient Analysis) Record your Prosperity Quotient below. Check it against your previous Quotient. Our own tests show that when people do not increase their score at this point, they generally have just skimmed through the Program. People who increase their scores really work with the Program—and why not?—when it can increase your income so tremendously!

My Prosperity Quotient on (date) _____ is _____

Psycho-Cybernetics

The Self Image Way to Get
More Living Out of Life

Look into a mirror and you see your outward image. Do you find that image acceptable? Maybe yes, maybe no.

But that outward image is nowhere near so important as the self image you carry within yourself—the face of your personality, so to speak, which is as handsome or as ugly as *you* make it. Moreover, it is your self image, not your outward face, which helps you either to achieve your goals—or lie down and give up.

Dr. Maxwell Maltz, a plastic surgeon, has changed many outward faces. He also has discovered, and proved, a method with which anyone can change the "face" of his personality and use that new, inward face as a positive guiding mechanism that steers

141

him toward success. The method, called Psycho-Cybernetics, gives you command of a kind of "mental surgery" with which you change your own self image to your own liking. This "mental surgery" is not only painless—it is exciting and enjoyable. You can use Psycho-Cybernetics every day and advance every day toward the goals you set up.

Man, in fact, is a goal-seeking creature, Dr. Maltz says. You need goals, and you are happier and healthier—let alone richer—when you attain them. Moreover, the goal-seeking instinct is so strong that all you need do is to set it to take you in the right direction. Your automatic steering mechanism, rooted in your personality, will do the rest.

"Free throws" show the principle in action

If you ever have played basketball, you know what a free throw is. You stand a certain distance from the basket and attempt to toss the ball into the basket. The more you practise free throws, the fewer baskets you will miss and the more baskets you will sink.

> A group of young men practised sinking free throws every day for 20 days. They were scored on the first day and the last day.
>
> A second group practised sinking free throws on the first day and the twentieth day of the same period, but they did not practise on the days between. They too were scored on the first day and the last day.
>
> A third group also practised sinking free throws on the first day and the twentieth day, with no *physical* practise on the days between. On all the days between, however, this group spent an equivalent time *imagining* they were throwing the ball into the basket. They went through all the motions and sensations of throwing the ball, but they did it inside their own minds—with their creative imaginations.

Let us look at the results:

The first group, which practised on all of the 20 days, showed a 24 per cent increase in their score.

The second group, which had no sort of interim practise, showed no improvement in their score.

The third group, which for 18 of the 20 days practised only in their imaginations, improved their score 23 per cent!

The goal of each group was the same—to improve their score in sinking free throws. Physical practise—or experience—did the trick for the group that steadily practised. But the equivalent experience was created by those who shot baskets in their imaginations—the experience was created in their imaginations—and they achieved essentially the same results.

To pin it down: That third group succeeded in giving themselves firm self images of goal-success. That is why they succeeded.

The "surgical instrument" that changes your self image, makes it what you want it to be, is your creative imagination.

Imagination and reality are not so far apart as you may think

Charles B. Roth, a great salesman and trainer of salesmen, taught his students how to sell with their self images. He had them play the role of selling in their imaginations even when they were not actually selling. They imagined themselves in various selling situations—confronted with various objections to buying, and so forth. They solved the attendant problems in their minds. Once the successful self image was firmly set up—once the automatic steering mechanism was adjusted toward *successful selling*—they went out and sold like wildfire.

Once there was a rather obscure chess player named Alekhine. He was not given much of a chance to beat the world's champion. He beat the champion nevertheless—after he had spent three months playing chess in his imagination.

As Dr. Harry Emerson Fosdick said: "Hold a picture of yourself long and steadily enough in your mind's eye and you will be drawn toward it."

Is it at all difficult to set the inner steersman of your personality? Can you really change from within and thus adjust the events of your life to your liking? Do you have to be a genius?

All you have to be is to be human. If you can remember, worry or tie your shoe, you can succeed.

What IS the image of a good, successful personality?

Having come so far in the Parker Prosperity Program, you know the value of setting up definite aims and ambitions. You know too that you must choose your goals for yourself.

Q: What is your main goal in life?

A: ———————————————— (only you can fill in the answer.)

The achievement of any goal, however, depends largely upon having a good "success type" personality. Within your personality, or self image, is where you find the basic building blocks that you build into one kind of achievement and another man builds into another.

"A good personality," says Dr. Maltz, "is one which enables you to deal effectively and appropriately with environment and reality, and to gain satisfaction from reaching goals which are important to you."

Let us break down this statement into its component parts. It is important in Psycho-Cybernetics to hold a graphic picture of what a "success type" personality looks like.

1. *Supply your guidance mechanism with a sense of direction*

> An advertising man in his early forties received an important and much-desired promotion. Immediately he felt insecure and dissatisfied with himself. He began to wonder what a small potato like himself was doing in such a big job.
>
> He became super-sensitive about his appearance, and thought his "weak chin" detracted from the appearance an executive should make. He asked Dr. Maltz to give him a "strong chin." Dr. Maltz saw this was not a case for the scalpel, but for the application of Psycho-Cybernetics. He showed the advertising man that his guidance mechanism had taken him to one goal, and he now had let it cut out completely instead of setting it for another. He had lost his sense of direction and so had damaged his personality; he was looking to someone else for direction—thinking now in terms of what *others* expected of *him*.

This man was made to see that new roles require some adjustment of the inner steersman. He made this adjustment and kept on going up.

Prescription Number One for developing a good personality: Always have something ahead of you to look forward to—to work for and hope for.

Functionally, a man is somewhat like a bicycle. A bicycle maintains its equilibrium only as long as it is moving, taking you somewhere.

2. Stay in good communication with your guidance system

You are not a machine. Your mind, however, acts like a computer in that it accepts information which it stores for later use. When your brain is well stored with guidance information—when the inner steersman always knows his course—small errors in course are quickly corrected.

We all realize we communicate constantly with others, but many of us do not realize how often we communicate with ourselves. Take an "others" situation as an example.

PERSONAL X-RAY

Is there some person you find difficult to "reach"? Some person with whom your communications always break down?

Ask yourself if the difficulty arises from nothing more than poor communication. Remember that the other fellow has his own set of values which you must take into account. What is perfectly clear to you may, to him, be completely muddy. A set of facts which, for you, point to only one conclusion, may point to an entirely different conclusion for him.

Poor communication—or directions—or instructions—cause just as much confusion when you give them to yourself. You cannot react appropriately to an event if the information you act upon is faulty or misunderstood. You cannot deal effectively with a problem if you do not have some understanding of its true nature. Carry this too far and you have a real neurosis in that you don't know where you are going—you are "all mixed up."

It is *essentially* a simple matter to feed appropriate directions into your mental computer—set up a true compass for your steersman to watch. What often gets in the way is the personality's "bad face." Bertrand Russell said one reason Hitler lost World War II was that he did not fully understand the situation. Bearers of bad news were punished. Soon no one dared tell Hitler the truth. Not knowing the truth, he could not act appropriately. And so it is even with men of good will who nevertheless fail because they'd rather let their steersman run on the rocks than feed in the information that a detour is necessary.

We simply do not like to admit to ourselves our errors, mistakes or shortcomings, or ever admit we may have been in the wrong. We rationalize too much—make events prove we were right *somehow.*

Prescription Number Two for developing a good personality: Seek out true information concerning yourself, your problems, other people's problems that affect you, and the factors that *really* govern situations you meet. Then you can build toward your goals on a better foundation than wishful thinking.

Especially, don't try to kid your inner steersman about obstacles in your path. Don't try to wish them away. We find no real satisfaction unless we have obstacles to overcome and goals to achieve on the other side.

3. *Make positive courage a strong and vital part of your personality*

Admiral William F. Halsey's motto was a quotation from Nelson: "No captain can do very wrong if he places his ship alongside that of an enemy."

General R. E. Chambers, Chief of the Army's Psychiatry and Neurology Consultant Division, said: "Most people don't know how brave they really are . . . many potential heroes live out their lives in self-doubt. If they only knew they had these deep resources, it would help give them the self-reliance to meet most problems, even a big crisis."

Strengthen your personality by acting boldly and with courage in regard to "little things." Do not wait till you can be a big hero in some dire crisis. Set up a courageous self image and the courage is there at any level of affairs.

Have you ever wondered why the desire to gamble seems to be inherent in human nature? Notice it; and notice, too, that those who ruin their lives at gambling tables often are people who refuse to live with creative courage—refuse, that is, to take the risks that go with living a creative life. A man who will not take a chance on himself simply perverts the natural instinct by finding something else to bet on; or he seeks courage from a bottle. Faith and courage are natural human instincts, and they are not far removed from gambling—of a constructive kind.

Now and then your well-instructed inner steersman *will* steer through a storm rather than go around it. And yet he has been well instructed nevertheless. Standing still, failing to act, can give you a lifetime of feeling stymied, trapped, paralyzed when facing the need for action. Even a step in the wrong direction is better than waiting to be pushed. Once you're moving forward, you can correct your course as you go.

Think of a self-guided missile which has its guidance computer set to take it to a certain target. Winds or other influences push it off course from time to time; but the error is fed into the computer and a correction is made. Even a machine can learn from its mistakes—and your mind is more wonderful than any machine that ever was invented. Have courage! Bet on *yourself*.

Prescription Number Three for developing a good personality: Don't sell yourself short. You have everything you need for success. But you never know the extent of your resources until you act— and give your resources a chance to work for you.

4. Consideration for others

It is a psychologic fact that our feelings about ourselves tend to correspond to our feelings about other people. When a person begins to feel more charitably toward others, he invariably begins to feel more charitably toward himself.

The person who feels that "people are not very important" cannot feel he himself is worthy of much respect and regard. He may reveal his inner inferiority by absolutely demanding that others kowtow to him—as with many an office dictator. You yourself are "people," and with what judgment you consider others, so are you unwittingly judged by the self image in your own mind. One of the best-known methods of getting over a feeling of guilt is to stop condemning other people even silently—stop judging them—stop blaming and hating them for their mistakes. You develop a better self image when you give more credit to the self image that every other person carries within himself.

A man who loves his wife kids her by saying, whenever she asks: "Do you love me?"—"Yes, whenever I stop to think about it." There is a lot of truth in this. We rarely feel one way or another about other people unless we stop and think about them. And a healthy self image will tell you every time that people are important and should be treated accordingly. Deal with others as though they were the human beings they are, rather than pawns in your own game.

Prescription Number Four for developing a good personality: Recognize that everyone you meet is, like yourself, a child of God. Cooperate with him. Treat him with dignity and respect.

5. *Maintain your self-esteem*

Thomas Carlyle had a thunderous temper, a waspish voice and was an appalling domestic tyrant. He gave himself away (to the modern psychologist) by remarking: "Alas! The fearful unbelief is unbelief in yourself."

His unbelief in himself is probably what drove this highly intelligent man to make himself unhappy and spread misery around him. A down-graded self image often shows itself by the noise it makes outside. Jealousy, for example, which is the scourge of many a marriage, is nearly always caused by corrosive self-doubt. The person who is "out to prove something"—generally that he is better than someone else—is a person whose self-esteem is at a woefully low level.

The word *esteem* literally means "to appreciate the worth of."

Why do men stand in awe of the stars, and the moon, the sea in its immensity, the beauty of a sunset, and at the same time downgrade themselves? Is not man himself the most marvelous creation of all?

Q: But what about humility? Is it not a virtue?

A: *That depends. A person of reasonable self-esteem can indeed show humility in that he does not consider himself basically better than anyone else. A Uriah Heep, forever " 'umble," is a sick creature, filled with hate.*

To appreciate your own worth is not raw egotism unless you assume that you created yourself and should take the credit. On the other hand, we have too many people who know they lack self-esteem but think it is inevitable because they are "not treated justly." Do not downgrade the product—your own illimitable mind —because you have not used it correctly. Don't childishly blame the product for your own lack of success like the schoolgirl who said: "This typewriter can't spell."

Prescription Number Five for developing a good personality: Stop carrying around any expression on the face of your personality that is an expression of defeat or lack of worth. Let your steersman know he has a captain whose average performance is really pretty good.

6. Build self-confidence into your personality

This ties in closely with Number Five. But here is another extremely important factor: *Self-confidence is built upon the experience of success.* Success breeds success—if you let it. Some people can do something a hundred times—quite well—yet never feel confidence in their ability to do it. Others, the ones with a healthy self image, simply expect to do well after the first few fumbles. This is true of speaking in public, riding a bicycle—any skill you care to name.

Here is the big difference: To build self-confidence, build upon your successes, not upon your failures. Practise, not only to achieve skill, but to confirm your hits—not your misses. "Repetition" has no value in itself. If it did, we would learn our errors as firmly as we learn the right way to do things—for you are bound to miss the basket now and then. Learn the right way and forget the wrong way. Initial experience teaches you both ways, but you have the extremely human privilege of learning by your mistakes.

Yet what do most of us do? We destroy our self-confidence by dwelling on our past failures and taking the attitude that our successes were in themselves a kind of mistake. We not only remember failures, but also we impress them on our minds with emotion. We condemn ourselves. We flay ourselves with shame and remorse —both of which are highly egotistical, self-centered emotions. And self-confidence disappears from the personality. It can find no place to live!

Amazingly enough, the mind often can nourish itself on the *feeling* of success as well as it can on the physical reality. Remember the group that practised free throws 18 days in their minds and only two days at the basket. They constantly formed the image of success—and when the time came, they lived up to that image. The same was true of the salesmen and of the chess player. The same has been shown to be true of people in every kind of occupation— and people of every age.

All of us have succeeded at something—be it cooking, be it winning the confidence of a child, be it painting a fence or what you will. All of us have "come through" on some really demanding occasions. Now remember the times you succeeded. Remember how you felt when you succeeded. The next time you are tempted to give in to the feeling best described as "I can't do it"—take a moment to recapture the feeling of success and you'll see you *can* do it. Especially when beginning a new task, call up the *feeling* you experienced in some past success, however small it may have been. The more self-confident you are, the more self-confident you will be.

Prescription Number Six for developing a good personality: Build self-confidence by building on success.

Why is this success method called psycho-cybernetics?

Perhaps you have recognized the word *cybernetics*. It came into the language not long ago, invented by Dr. Norbert Weiner, a pioneer in modern computer methods. It is derived from the Greek word for *steersman,* and refers particularly to the ability of some computers to make their own adjustments while in operation. We mentioned how this works in a self-guided missile: the goal is set into the missile's computer (or is picked up by some sensing device as the missile proceeds) and any deviation from the goal is treated as an error. This deviant reading is fed back into the computer, which adjusts the course, and thus the missile is steered.

Psycho-Cybernetics, then, is the application of the steersman idea to the far more complex human mind, and to human affairs, through practical self image psychology. A self image of failure steers you toward failure; a self image of success steers you toward success.

Q: But can't an ugly or disfigured *outward* face steer you toward failure?

A: *Yes it can, if you are dreadfully ugly or horribly disfigured. In that case, a plastic surgeon can help you feel more self-confident and accepted by giving you a better face to show to the world. Yet, in many cases, such face-rebuilding does not change "the face of the personality." Remember the man who thought he did not look like an executive because he had what he called a weak chin. All he needed was to give himself an executive's face inside.*

How to unlock your best personality

How do you find that good, successful personality whose image we have shown in words? How do you set up a self image which helps you reach *any* goal when you say that goal is yours—and you mean it?

You release that personality—unlock it—unchain it—from within yourself.

The person with a "poor personality" simply does not allow himself to express his great, creative self. For one reason or another he is afraid to break loose and become what he could be.

A certain salesman always managed to make almost exactly $5,000 a year. In a poor territory he made $5,000; when he was

given a really "hot" territory, and an increased commission rate besides, he still earned the same.

Once, when this man had earned $5,000 before the end of the
year, he got sick and was unable to work. Doctors could find nothing wrong with him. On the first day of the next year he made a
miraculous recovery! And he went on to earn precisely $5,000 that
year.

In effect, this man was self-hypnotized. Somewhere, somehow he
had picked up the deep belief that he was a $5,000-a-year man, and
that was the barrier he could not break . . . did not want to break,
even became ill rather than break it. Few cases are so dramatically
clear, but all such cases are basically alike. The repression or inhibition of the best self takes root somehow and there it sits,
shading and choking what could be a good self image.

Too much inhibition; the steersman takes over

You are the captain of your soul, as the well-known saying goes,
and so *you*, as captain, set your goal, then tell your inner steersman
to take you to it. His job is to correct your course, if necessary,
while you are on your way. But you are *on your way*.

When you smother your best personality, however, your steersman is not saying: "You're not proceeding correctly; here's a better
course." He says: "You're all wrong. Stop. Give up."

That's what inhibition does. And even when you know nothing
of a man's record, you can spot an inhibited personality. You can
see the self image. You can assume he isn't going anywhere, and in
most cases you will be right.

Simple personality pep-ups that break
the chains of inhibition

The following methods may seem to be too simple—but they work.
They change the self image to a surprising degree; place the self
image where the sun can shine on it.

Notice that these methods amount to "bending over backward"
to correct inhibition; but don't worry, in the end you stand very
straight.

1. *Don't wonder in advance what you are going to say. Just open your mouth and say it.*

This seems to be contrary to other advice you've heard, and it may at times get you into a "situation." But hear this: What a person says after long cogitation and what he says "off the top of his head" generally are not far apart. So *say it*—don't choke it back down your throat. The very act of finding yourself speaking causes you to think faster and with less inhibition. The very act of drawing attention to yourself shows you that being noticed isn't so bad after all.

2. *Make a habit of speaking louder than usual.*

Inhibited people are notoriously soft-spoken. Raise the volume of your voice; fill your lungs with air before you speak and let the bellows action of your diaphragm get behind the words you form distinctly in the front of your mouth. You don't have to shout. Notice how many people always speak so that everyone in range can hear them—and *you* think nothing of it. Speak *up*—it soon becomes natural—and you soon begin to enjoy the world as a place in which you *express yourself.*

3. *"Take no thought for tomorrow."*

Or little thought, at any rate. The important thing is: Get into action without the overdone planning and the over-worried cogitating which is so characteristic of inhibited people. Try *not* thinking before you act, and you'll find—as with not planning what you are going to say—that once you are committed to a situation, reserves of ingenuity and purpose spring into action to help you handle it.

This is anciently known. Once again turning to the Bible, we may note the advice of Jesus to give no thought as to what we would say if delivered up to councils, but allow the spirit to advise us what to say at that time.

And it ties right in with cybernetics. The guided device does not (and cannot) think out all of its possible errors in advance. It must act first—start moving toward its goal—then correct errors which may occur. "We cannot think first and act afterwards," said

A. N. Whitehead. "From the moment of birth we are immersed in action, and can only fitfully guide it by taking thought."

4. *Stop criticising yourself.*

The inhibited person is typically self-critical. Even after he acts—reluctantly—he says to himself: "I wonder if I should have *done* that." Or *said* that. He is overloaded with the wrong kind of conscience—he has the wrong basic beliefs about what is right and what is wrong. Self-criticism and self-analysis is good and useful when it is undertaken quite consciously, done well, then put aside. As a daily habit it frustrates you. As a moment-to-moment habit it throws and ropes you. It is in no way wrong to let your conscience be your guide so long as you remember that the purpose of conscience is to help make us happy and productive—not the other way around.

5. *Let people know you like them.*

This is very basic.

The inhibited person is as afraid of expressing "good" feelings as bad ones. If he expresses love, he is afraid it will be judged as sentimentality. If he expresses friendship, he is afraid it will be considered fawning. If he compliments someone he is afraid that person will think him superficial, or suspect an ulterior motive.

The inhibited person is *afraid.* It shows in scores of ways. And this simple area of personal relations exerts great leverage upon the fears that go along with inhibition.

Express your friendship! Express your appreciation of good work done, even of a good try. Notice the other fellow's new suit or pretty dress and put your notice on the record. Express love, especially, and more than once a day. Open your shell and watch other people open theirs. Tell other people in one way or another that they are important in your world—and lo, you find out *you* are important to *them.* Show them the face of your personality as a pleasant face, and you help your inner face find all kinds of happy expression.

Can you do it? Of course you can, because nothing, absolutely nothing is stopping you—except yourself.

Can you see that now? NOBODY INHIBITS YOU EXCEPT YOURSELF

We are not concerned here with tracking down where your inhibition may have come from. Once you have it, it is yours. Once it is yours, you can deal with it. And you'll never know your power to unlock your real, good personality—until you try.

An experiment with stutterers showed how much their inhibition of speech was a *self*-inhibition:

> Twenty-five severe stutterers were asked to read aloud. Everyone stuttered badly and made a mess of his reading. Then each was equipped with earphones through which a loud tone drowned out the sound of their own voices. Now, when asked to read aloud, they showed a remarkable improvement—because *they could not hear themselves*. Therefore they were removed from the rationale of their constant self-criticism of their poor speech which only made matters worse. To put it another way: when these stutterers were removed from the evidence of their own failure, they were able to make at least a near approach to success.

To put it yet another way: each of them gave his inner steersman at least a chance to steer him toward the goal of acceptable speech. Each stutterer remained physically the same, but he was able to "get away from himself"—and a better self was waiting to take over.

Fear is what scars your self image. Nobody is immune to fear. But is fear merely one of your large catalog of emotions—or your major emotion? That is where the difference comes in.

General George Patton, the hell-for-leather general of World War II fame, once was asked if he ever experienced fear before a battle. Yes, he said, he often experienced fear. But, he added, "I never take counsel of my fears."

One person feels fear and simply handles it—doesn't let it give orders to his steersman. Another, feeling fear, takes it as a "sure sign" that he will fail—which of course is a great aid in failing.

PERSONAL X-RAY

Which kind of person are you?

That "winning feeling" is controlled
by rational thinking

Until you really try, you can have no idea of your power to turn your conscious, rational thoughts away from failure—and away from the memory of failure—and toward the confident expectation of success.

And while the personality does have its mysteries—while there does appear to be a subconscious mind—it is conscious, rational thinking that eventually forms the neuron patterns of habit. Thoughts *you control* can give you the habit of living according to that "winning feeling."

The late Dr. John A. Schindler won fame for his success in helping unhappy, neurotic people regain the joy of living and return to productive, happy lives. His percentage of cures far exceeded that of psychoanalysis. One of his key methods of treatment was *conscious thought control*. He said:

> "Regardless of the omissions and commissions of the past, a person has to start in the present to acquire some maturity so that the future may be better than the past. The present and the future depend on learning new habits and new ways of looking at old problems . . . . the underlying emotional factor has the same common denominator in every patient. This common denominator is that the patient has forgotten how, or probably never learned how, to control his *present thinking* to produce enjoyment." *

There it is again; the recognition that the habit of turning the mind toward old failures and old mistakes is what prevents the mind from forming new patterns of happiness.

WHAT ARE YOU GOING TO DO ABOUT IT—
RATIONALLY AND CONSCIOUSLY?

1. Don't prepare to fail; prepare to succeed

A man failed in business several times. The first time he failed, it

---

* John A. Schindler, *How To Live 365 Days a Year*, Englewood Cliffs, N.J., Prentice-Hall, Inc., 1954.

took him a long time to pay the debts he had incurred. Thereafter, he was afraid to gather sufficient capital, afraid to lay in enough reserve stock, and he never really "acted as though he were in business," as his wife complained. He kept on failing, and always for the same reasons. At last he learned how to re-think the entire matter of going into business, and this time he started a company with enough capital and his mind free of fear that he would fail again. He spent sufficient money on making his store attractive, on advertising, on getting the right kind of help. He also was cheerful and confident in dealing with his customers, and acted in every way as though he had a good business and knew it. He did not fail, and soon could honestly call himself a success.

Any person who wants to show he has a record of failure can show it. We all make plenty of mistakes. But no mistake you ever made can affect today's success *if you don't let it.* The steersman always will accept new orders, but not till you cancel the old orders which went something like: "We've gone on the rocks so many times, we had better expect to go on the rocks again."

Your mind is not a phonograph record, permanently grooved with a sad song you must play over and over. There aren't any "grooves" at all—just patterns of thought that conscious thought can change . . . conscious thoughts of confidence, success, achievement and happiness.

2. Remember the value of role-playing

The young men who successfully shot baskets in their minds, the salesmen who sold in their creative imaginations, the chess player who first beat the champion in his thoughts—all were playing roles. That they had failed in the past did not concern them. They played the role of success and won success.

Hypnosis offers convincing proof that *playing a role* is closely allied to *being* what you want to be. A shy, timid wallflower, faced with the necessity of making a speech, can be hypnotized so that his attention is given over completely to the desired goal. He makes a great speech because nothing prevents him from being what he believes he is.

A woman wanted to be a writer, but found it almost impossible to write with any degree of ease. She witnessed such a demonstration of hypnosis. Then she happened to read a psychologist's statement that the latent talents brought to the surface by hypnotic subjects were due to a "purgation of memory." Instead of remembering their past failures, and being inhibited by them, they "started from scratch."

If this were possible, the woman asked herself, why couldn't a person in a wakeful state also ignore past failures and "act as if it were impossible to fail." She determined to act on the assumption that the ability to write fluently and well *was there*, and needed only to be used. She acted *as if* in every possible way—and within a year her writing production and her income had increased many times.

You too can play a role.

What role should you play? *The Person I Want to Be.*

If the person you want to be is quite different from the person you have been—so much the better.

3. Examine and re-evaluate your beliefs

Ideas are changed, not by "will," but by other ideas. Are you wedded to some deep belief that does you harm? Stamp it out by putting a good, constructive belief in the same place.

One of Dr. Maltz's patients was a salesman who was scared to death when he called on men who wielded big business power. His basic belief—or fear—was that he might not win their approval.

Dr. Maltz asked the salesman: "Would you go into a man's office with your hand out like a beggar's, whining for a dime for a cup of coffee?"

"Certainly not!"

"But you are doing essentially the same thing. You are literally begging him to approve of you and accept you."

The salesman, after one counselling session, replaced his belief in his own unworthiness with a perfectly obvious belief that one man is as good as another. He had no trouble after that.

While there are many damaging beliefs, the belief of unworthiness—the belief that you are really not entitled to the best in life—is basic in most unsuccessful personalities.

PERSONAL X-RAY

Does "something always happen" to cause me to miss out on success—over and over?

Do I tend to make a virtue of having tried and not having succeeded? Do I want just as much credit for having tried?

Do I neglect to go through the obvious motions indicated for a particular success? (Like the man who kept on starting businesses with insufficient capital)

Do I generally keep company with unsuccessful people?

Do I tend to find faults in people who have demonstrated their success?

If you answer *Yes* to most of those questions, you probably have formed self-defeating habits of preparing for failure instead of for success. You may also be making a virtue of failure—trying to make yourself "look right" somehow—even trying to rationalize that somehow it is unworthy to win success.

Examine these beliefs. You'll see how badly they affect one's self image.

YOU CAN ALWAYS CHANGE YOUR MIND
ABOUT YOURSELF

And when you change your mind, will your mind change *you?* You bet it will!

Get in touch with that inner steersman. Use every method shown here. Make sure your *cybernete* knows where you want to go. And use your creative imagination in every possible way to see yourself going there . . . and arriving.

Your course will vary very little. You will win goal after goal.

Psycho-Emotive Reminders:

You may or may not approve of your physical face—
but it is your "inner face" that either helps you achieve

your goals or makes you fail. A kind of mental surgery called Psycho-Cybernetics can change the "face of your personality" and instruct your inner "steersman" to steer you toward your own chosen success.

Your creative imagination is your "surgical instrument." Let it show you to yourself as a successful person. Build a good, successful personality by giving your inner steersman a sense of direction—by staying in touch with the guidance system that corrects your errors—by making courage your guiding principle—by having consideration for others so that you do not sully your own opinion of yourself—by maintaining your self-esteem without false humility—by building upon your experience of success, never upon failure, to win the self-confidence that makes you *go*.

To unlock your successful personality, get rid of inhibition. Develop certain habits which have terrific inhibition-breaking power: Don't worry too much about what you are going to say, but say it—make a habit of speaking louder than usual—"take no thought for tomorrow" in the sense that you realize you are always immersed in action —develop the talent of letting people know you like them—and above all, realize that nobody inhibits you except yourself.

The *winning feeling* is yours when you prepare to succeed, not to fail. You can play a role, telling yourself that you have what it takes to succeed, then going ahead with complete confidence.

My Personal Notes on Lesson Seven:

Suggestions:

Ask your local librarian for any book of reminiscences by any plastic surgeon. See if Doctor X remarks—as he probably does—on the way people blame their outward faces for their failure, when it is their personalities that hold them back.

Watch for this phenomenon in people you know. (Including yourself)

Record any story, "Q & A" of Personal X-ray which has special meaning for you. Remember, there is a reason for any special meaning that comes through. Think about it.

List some mistakes you have made in the past year. Then list, with each mistake, how you acted afterward. Did you steer yourself according to the correction you could have won from the mistake? Or did you steer yourself straight toward making the same mistake again?

The next lesson is based on interviews with 3,000 individuals. It shows why many of them missed a powerful new shortcut to personal success—and how a system of Dynamic Thinking sets you firmly on this shorter, better road to money, power, influence, security and happiness.

Dynamic Thinking

A Powerful New Shortcut to Personal Success

WHAT IS THE ONE BASIC INGREDIENT that separates the successful person from the run-of-the-mill individual?

What is it that makes a man no smarter—but far more effective . . . no taller—but far more impressive . . . no luckier—but far more wealthy . . . and also far more happy in his business life and in his personal life as well?

Knowing what you want out of life.

Robert J. O'Reilly has interviewed more than 3,000 aspirants for success—and saw this factor in about two per cent of the persons he interviewed. Yet nobody denies this factor is indispensable for success. It is just that so few people are willing to come to grips with it, put dynamic thinking behind it, put *themselves* behind it with all the latent power that can take any man where he wants to go.

Only two per cent of the people Mr. O'Reilly interviewed knew what they wanted out of life. And until you know what you want, you not only cannot get what you want—which is obvious—but also you are not likely to get anything very good.

Mr. O'Reilly's system, *Dynamic Thinking*, contains some unique approaches to this truth which is so widely recognized. Some of his methods are made to be personalized to your own needs. Other methods set up the basic qualities that spark and vitalize any man's drive to success.

WHY IS *TOMORROW-ITIS* SUCH A COMMON DISEASE?

The majority of unsuccessful people suffer from tomorrow-itis— which means that most people suffer from tomorrow-itis. It's a very comfortable disease to rationalize yourself into because, after all, tomorrow always comes.

In Eugene O'Neill's play, *The Iceman Cometh*, a saloon keeper named Harry Hope has spent 20 years without setting foot outside his own door. He always *means* to go out. In fact, his proposed "walk around the block" has become an obsession with him. But he's busy. Or the weather is bad, or he finds a dozen other reasons to stay home, and go tomorrow.

So Harry Hope's "tomorrows" added up to two decades. And many of those who give a pitying smile to the fictional Harry Hope are, in reality, adding up their tomorrows until far too many have gone by and nothing has been done.

If you are dissatisfied with the opportunities offered in your present job, how long have you put off making the change?

If you feel you deserve a raise or a promotion, how long have you put off asking for it and showing why it should be yours?

That new hobby? That long-deferred trip? How long will you delay enjoying them?

That self-improvement program on which you have so long intended to embark? Are you doing more than reading about it? Are you working on it *now?*

Tomorrow-itis is a deadly habit. Like any of our other habits, it begins simply and innocently enough with our consent. In a little while, however, the habit takes over. The longer you live with it, the harder it is to break.

The time to cure yourself of tomorrow-itis is not tomorrow, but now. Don't read on until you have searched yourself for the danger signals.

PERSONAL X-RAY

Read over this list of danger signals. They are very ordinary phrases. Read the list several times, till you are familiar with each phrase. Then notice how many of them creep into your vocabulary —spoken or unspoken.

"I've been too busy to get around to it. . . ."
"I haven't had a chance to do it. . . ."
"I'll do it as soon as I have some free time. . . ."
"Sure I can do it, but I have other things to do. . . ."
"I think I'll rest up a bit before I start. . . ."
"I've been wanting to do it, but. . . ."
"I'll do it tomorrow. . . ."

Some of those phrases are bound to sound familiar. We all are guilty of *some* procrastination. Sometimes—just *sometimes*—your use of one of those phrases may be justified. The decisive factor is: Do you find yourself conditioned to using those strangling phrases in regard to important decisions? If so, the deadly habit has reached the critical point. It has become a towering roadblock on the avenue of success.

How to break the stranglehold of tomorrow-itis

At this point you may be saying: "But my case is different. I really don't have the time to do the things I want to do."

This only points up the first of the two real causes of tomorrow-itis: indifference. "Tomorrow" is your labor-saving device—and probably you don't know what you're working for, anyway.

A speaker at the New York Sales Executive Club hammered down this point. "Suppose," he said, "the president of your company called you in, showed you a huge pile of thousand-dollar bills, and told you that you could keep every bill you could count between 9 A.M. and 5 P.M. How much time would you take for lunch that day? Why, you wouldn't even take time out to go to the bathroom!"

Once you accept the fact that you simply do not motivate yourself toward great accomplishment—so naturally you don't get started—it's like snapping on a bright light in a dark cellar. You stop groping. You stop giving up trying. You see what you want and you go straight to it.

Question yourself about your own indifference

The questions can be in your own words, but they should follow this pattern:

1. Why am I so indifferent about achieving success in (whatever area it may be)? It must be indifference, or lack of interest, or certainly I would have taken some definite action by now. Lack of time is nothing more than an excuse—look at the unimportant, menial matters to which I give so much time every day. Surely, if I really wanted to, I could re-allocate some of this time and really make it do something for me. So, if there is no real interest in achieving this, let's just forget about it and move on to more important things.

Talking things over with yourself requires complete honesty! Given this honesty, you will arrive at some conclusion. You may very well find that you are not really indifferent. Go on questioning:

2. No, it can't be indifference because this is something I am vitally interested in achieving. It is really important to me. Then what's taking me so long to do something about it? Why do I keep putting it off in favor of less important things? WHAT AM I AFRAID OF? Possibly I'm unsure of my ability in this area.

Maybe I'm risking too much if I should fail. Whatever it is, let's drag it out into the open, carefully evaluate it, and see what to do about it.

And that's when you find out that when you bring your fears out into the open, you can grapple with them. And when you start grappling, they no longer seem so strong.

In many a case, one or both of these steps is sufficient to shift tomorrow-itis' stranglehold and give *you* a stranglehold on tomorrow-itis. But in all events, when you know you suffer from the habit of tomorrow-itis, take steps to break the habit. By far the easiest and surest way is to replace it with an opposite habit.

How to get into the habit of doing it now

Probably you do not have to make important decisions every day. Every day, however, you make dozens of small decisions, or call them simply actions you either decide to do or decide to put off. A small repair "around the house"? Calling a friend you haven't seen in quite a while? Answering a letter that's been lying around? Starting a book you've wanted to read? Putting in a little extra time to get caught up on work?

Do it now. At least, today. While the literal "now" may at times show some physical impossibility, you can schedule a time, and when that time comes—sometime today—it is *now*. You'll phone your friend, say, at nine o'clock, when you know he comes home from night school. Nine o'clock becomes *now*.

Sometimes we do not start tasks because we know we cannot finish them the same day, so they begin to look mountainous. As Peter Marshall said: "Small deeds done are better than great deeds planned." Get started!

Keep your mind focused on the main issue—the habit which is to replace the bad habit of procrastination—the habit so well described as DO IT NOW. The *do*, at this stage, is more important than the *it*—and the *now* is all-important.

Work that is rewarded helps you keep working and work better. Your almost-instant reward will be the wonderful feeling of *getting things accomplished*. You will like yourself more—and that is a very valuable feeling. After a few weeks of doing it now, you'll feel as though somebody had lifted a tremendous weight from your mind. And a tremendous psychological weight has been removed. For the first time you will have gotten rid of trivial, petty details that bog down your thinking and action.

Let us move a step onward and consider some matter that really will take "doing." That's where tomorrow-itis, not quite conquered, can move in and once more take over. All right—do this:

Make it progressively more difficult NOT to do what needs to be done

> Julius Caesar sailed over from Gaul (now France) and landed with his legions in what is now England. When he had got his men to the top of the chalk cliffs of Dover, the men became aware of a great fire on the shore, at the foot of the cliffs. The ships which had brought them across the Channel were burning! Caesar had set fire to them. Now the legions had no means of retreat. There was only one thing left to do—advance and conquer. That is exactly what they did.

Such drastic procedures are not necessarily to be recommended in every case, but the point is clear. We tend to take the line of least resistance, which is *not* getting things done. Make it difficult, therefore, not to do it.

One good way is to obligate yourself to other people. Go out of your way to tell them: "I am going to do so and so by a certain date." Repeat it. Make sure they definitely expect some definite performance by you, and not merely "sometime," but by a certain deadline. You'll find it so difficult to back off, so much more pleasant to get it done, that you'll go out of your way to do it.

Another good way is to leave written reminders for yourself in several conspicuous spots—such as pasted on your shaving mirror, clipped onto the sun visor of your car, and so forth. Just to get rid of those nagging reminders, you'll go ahead and do it.

Where do I find the time?

That can be a perfectly honest question. It's the various answers which often tend not to look facts in the face!

Nobody has unlimited time. Nobody, in fact, has any more time than anyone else. Nobody can squeeze more than 60 minutes into an hour or more than 24 hours into a day. Which only points up the fact that time is so valuable you cannot put a price on it. The busy man who says: "My time is money" is only making an approach to the truth.

Well, where *do* you find the time, when you *can* show in black and white that all your time is taken up and you still are getting nowhere?

You read, understand and follow this highly important time-management principle:

The best way to make time available is to
displace other, less important time.

Q: Who is to say whether or not I am spending my time importantly? I am the only one who can judge that.

A: *That's right, you are the only one who can judge. But what criteria do you judge by? Look at the criteria as well as the hours.*

To begin with, here is how a national magazine broke down the way an average worker spends his time in a week—that's 168 hours.

40 hours	Work
56 hours	Sleep
10 hours	Transportation
7 hours	Personal Grooming
10½ hours	Dining
44½ hours	Leisure

168

Give or take a bit in each category, this seems a fair all-around picture. Now let us divide that week into three special categories:

Category "A"—Inflexible Time

Work	40 hours
Personal Grooming	7 hours
Dining	10½ hours

Category "B"—Semi-Flexible Time
Sleep .... 56 hours
Transportation .... 10 hours

Category "C"—Completely Flexible Time
Leisure .... 44½ hours

Now let's examine Category "A". This kind of time is pretty well taken up. True, you probably could chop a few minutes off the second two items—but we're not out to live a Spartan existence. Let us say it is not a good idea to skimp on grooming or rush through meals.

In Category "B" you have to be your own judge. If you are a normally healthy person, there probably is no sound reason why you couldn't get along on a half-hour's less sleep every night, or even an hour's—if not every night, then at least every other night. This would "find" anywhere from 1½ to 7 hours of extra, valuable time every week. (More about sleep later)

Transportation? While this is a necessary daily item for many workers, in many cases we can do two things at once. If we are driving, it is possible to do some creative thinking during the trip. A passenger can do the same, or read if conditions permit. Quite a few hours can be "found" by this time-displacement, and it is up to you to see whether it can be done. As Henry Ford observed: "Many people get ahead during the time others waste."

Category "C" is where we hit the jackpot. It deserves special treatment.

YOUR LEISURE TIME AND YOUR SUCCESS:
THE MAGIC SIXTY MINUTES

Go back and look at that figure for average leisure time per week. Forty-four and a half hours! Anyone who says he can't displace and use at least 7 hours a week from this category alone, just isn't being honest with himself.

True, it may mean missing some of your favorite TV shows, or maybe a movie or a ball game. But remember what Emerson once said: "For everything you have missed, you have gained something else." And many a person finds out that when he takes time off his "TV time" he becomes more choosy about the TV shows he does take time to watch—so he gains in both directions.

Be that as it may, you don't need much time in which to lift yourself completely out of the rut of mediocrity. Many a man has done it in as little as 60 minutes a day.

An hour a day spent in finding out about a proposition offered to you, or a new business, or a new job can show you a great deal. And it takes away your fear of making a change because now you know what lies ahead of you. Or you don't make the change—and you still build your self-confidence because you know you did right.

An hour a day spent in training yourself or getting training in some skill or in some area of knowledge can qualify you for a better job, help you make more out of your present job, make you an expert in some subject in a surprisingly short time. This may seem incredible, but the fact is that *we have very few experts* in business because so few men are willing to be expert.

A man whose "time is money" and can see the definite correlation can lift his income at least 17.5 per cent by working the extra seven hours. (7 divided by 40) Generally the gain will be much more, as has been shown in practise.

In that hour every day you can pursue some special study or work on some favorite idea or invention. In this manner, many a man has made more money than he ever could have made in his 8 hours at his regular job.

And if you begin to feel sorry for yourself, or if anyone feels sorry for you because you are "working so hard"—take firm notice of your 37½ hours of leisure per week—which would have seemed an impossible amount of free time for the average worker 30 years ago.

Where will I find the energy?

You have it.

Get it focused. Your goal is your focus. What you want out of life is your focus—both for your time and your energy. Merely to know where you are going puts a great charge into your physical battery. Achieving your main goal through the attainment of interim goals gives you a booster charge every time you "get there."

PERSONAL X-RAY

Let us look more deeply into this matter of energy.

> Just as you did in the case of tomorrow-itis, check yourself to see how many of these anti-energy phrases creep into your vocabulary—spoken or unspoken:
>
> "I've seen what the rat race for success can do to you. I'd rather stay poor and keep my health."
>
> "I'm exhausted now at the end of a day. It isn't possible for me to do any more."
>
> "If I cut down on the amount of sleep I get, I'd hardly be able to get up in the morning. I'd end up by being groggy all day."
>
> "Sure I'd like a promotion, but *that* job would take too much out of me. I don't have the energy to make an executive."
>
> "Some people were born with energy. I wasn't, and that's all there is to it."

Such statements may sound true because you have heard them so often from yourself and others. There is very little truth in any of them.

They go back to that very human failing of rationalization, or finding reasons to prove you are right. You are offered an advancement and you don't want it because you are too lazy. You *say*, however—and force yourself to believe—"No thanks, you can keep those top jobs with their built-in ulcers. I have no intention of becoming a nervous wreck for just a few extra bucks a week."

Well, let's look at a conclusion reached by Dr. Gerald Gordon, chief psychiatrist of E. I. Du Pont de Nemours & Company:

> The popular notion that executive work is inherently a man-killing rat race which only a few hardy souls can endure has been flatly repudiated by a careful series of studies begun by the Du Pont Medical Division . . . and since repeated in several other leading companies. These studies show that the incidence of stress-related

diseases among managers . . . is not appreciably greater than in any other segment of the population . . . The man who seeks false tranquility by running away from problems is far more likely to develop dangerous inner stresses than the one who works . . . until the problem is solved.

What about relative length of life? The National Office of Vital Statistics studied the differences in death rates at every income level. Their findings showed that the biggest money-makers—professional men, business executives, senior technical personnel—generally live longer than lower-income office workers, salesmen, skilled and semi-skilled workers, laborers, and small proprietors.

And the records of 19 insurance companies for the years 1934-1953 show lower death rates for large policyholders—usually successful men—than for small. So perhaps the executive who dies at his desk simply gets more notice than does a lower-level man.

An experiment in sleep that can open a gold mine of time and energy for you

We spoke of time, we spoke of time spent in sleep, now we are speaking of energy—and we come back to sleep because most men connect sleep with energy. This is true, of course, in that you must sleep in order to restore your energy. But the man who really needs time can find a gold mine of time by displacing hours from his sleeping time into productive time—and he may be even more energetic.

Sleep tends to become very sacred. Here is where you really need Dynamic Thinking!

First of all, here is a "Q & A" section based on studies at the Dream and Sleep Research Project at the University of Chicago:

Q: How much sleep does a person need?

A: *There is no standard amount of sleep which everyone requires. Among adults, the amount varies anywhere from 5 to 9 or 10 hours a night. Knowing the average—7.5 hours—doesn't help you. You wouldn't buy a pair of shoes because they were average size.*

Q: How do you tell how much sleep you need?

A: *Vary the amount and see the effect, but give yourself several days in which to become adjusted to each variation.*

Q: If you wake up groggy, reluctant to get out of bed, does that mean you are not getting enough sleep?

A: *Not necessarily. Body efficiency seems to operate in cycles. It is generally at a low ebb just before we go to bed and just after we awaken.*

Q: If you miss some sleep, do you have to catch up on every hour you have missed?

A: *No. A couple of hours of extra sleep will correct a sleep deprivation of several nights' standing.*

Q: Are there psychological reasons for sleeping more than we have to—and claiming we *do* have to sleep that much?

A: *Yes! People who dislike their jobs, or want someone else to fix breakfast, find they "must" sleep later in the morning. The same people will be out of bed with the birds, full of pep, when something pleasant and exciting is promised.*

There you have a pretty good picture of what goes on in the too-sacred realm of sleep.

Think about this: If you should uncover just one extra hour a day from your "sleep" category, that will amount to the equivalent of 45 full 8-hour bonus days in the course of a year. And that is equal to 9 full working weeks in a year—in addition to time you gain by displacing a little from your leisure!

And of course we are interested into turning waking hours into productive hours—not just seeing how long you can stay awake without collapsing.

Chart your sleep and build your productivity

Here is the experiment that can help you feel better, do more, and earn more on less sleep—and have more energy left over for fun.

First: Buy yourself a diary. The experiment will take about seven weeks, so mark off at least seven weeks in the diary. Let's say you are going to start experimenting with nine hours of sleep every night for a week, then cut it down by half-hour decrements to six hours. Rule each "experiment page" with a chart like this:

Monday — December 4th
9 hour per night week

	VERY TIRED	TIRED	AVERAGE	ALERT	VERY ALERT
Immed. on arising					
At work 9 A.M.					
At work 11 A.M.					
At work 2 P.M.					
At work 4 P.M.					
Immed. after work					
After dinner					
Before retiring					

EXACT TIME WENT TO BED LAST NIGHT ......

EXACT TIME WOKE UP THIS MORNING ....

A couple of sheets of carbon paper will help you get the ruling done quickly. Each page will bear its own printed date. Under the date, note: *9 hour per night week, 8½ hour per night week,* and so forth.

Each day, you simply put a check mark next to how you felt at that particular time. Here are three important rules to follow:

1. You are to sleep exactly the amount of hours allotted. Any variances will distort the result. Use a reliable alarm clock throughout the experiment. If you should wake up before the alarm goes off, remain in bed and try to drift back to sleep.
2. Record the check marks as close to the indicated time each day as possible. If you ever are prevented from doing this, note the time you actually checked.
3. Maintain a psychological consistency in evaluating *tired, average, alert* and so forth. If at one time you use snap judgment in deciding how you feel, don't, at another time, take ten minutes in making the same decision. (Snap judgment will do in any event.)

Is your sticktoitiveness equal to following this routine faithfully for seven weeks? If you find yourself saying—"Ah, the hell with it" —ask yourself if you really are interested in gaining 9 full working weeks a year, every year. That should keep you at it. After a week or two you will find you have created a daily habit pattern of checking off your chart, and the procedure will become almost unnoticeable. Get started!

Get swinging on this experiment in sleep and you'll find it's not work—it's an exciting game. After a few days you begin to see patterns forming on your charts. Since you don't know how the patterns will turn out, nor how they will change when you go onto next week's schedule, your interest will increase as you go along. And when you find yourself enjoying a breakthrough—realizing, perhaps, that you are just as energetic after dinner on 7 hours of sleep as you ever were on 8 hours—you'll recommend this sleep experiment to all your friends.

You end with a truly scientific report on how much sleep YOU need. And more. You can relate your energy ups and downs to certain times of the day and perhaps rearrange your affairs to give yourself a rest break at those periods. (But notice too that when you are doing something really interesting and rewarding, you'll go right through one of those periods and never miss the break you didn't take!)

You'll also find that "missing sleep" can pass off just as "missing food" does when you go on a diet. You just have to give yourself a chance to get used to it; then you find you didn't need the extra hours/calories after all.

The post-graduate course: Push back your fatigue times

Once you really know the minimum amount of sleep you need for YOUR optimum efficiency, you can get your so-called fatigue periods down to practically nothing.

(You will realize by then that extra, self-indulgent hours of sleep do *not* get rid of fatigue periods. You will know it by your own experience, which is better than merely reading it in a book.)

And if you are in the right job you surely will have noticed the phenomenon mentioned a few paragraphs ago—that fatigue periods tend to disappear when something really interesting is going on.

Now take notice that *we get used to being tired at certain times.* Take quitting time. Watch people slumping and grumping out the door. Try walking briskly, with your head up, smiling, when you leave your place of work. You'll feel better instantly no matter how much "reason" you may have for being tired.

Do this: Once you have seen the pattern of your fatigue periods—*break the pattern.* Push back each fatigue period half an hour. Just keep going at that time. When you've pushed it back half an hour, push it back another half hour. There is no place for these fatigue periods to go after you've pushed them right down to the time when you go to sleep. It may sound incredible, but a person with a healthy attitude toward work and toward success and toward life can almost eliminate fatigue that is not due to actual physical labor.

Why not, after all? *Most of your fatigue begins inside your own head,* where you may not have enough interest in your work and enough sense of what you want out of life to keep your energy going.

Determine what success means to you

Think dynamically, actively, and absolutely honestly about success. Cast aside all the clichés about what success is and isn't. Think of the things that give YOU personal satisfaction. Maybe it's painting a picture or building something in your workshop. Maybe it's the thrill of closing a big sale. Perhaps it's the boost you get out of outsmarting the stock market.

When you have honestly decided what really moves *you*—make a list of the factors. There may be two lists, one that pertains to your livelihood, and one that pertains to your avocations. Get a clear picture! Don't work in the dark.

Suppose you clearly and honestly discover that you never have had a job that really interested you, but your hobbies or sidelines are what you really live for. All right—how about turning a hobby or a sideline into a profitable business?

Risky? Of course. But isn't it worth the risk? You can earn a living and enjoy yourself at the same time. You can feel you are using your best qualities most productively.

A survey reported in *This Week* said: "A nationwide survey of men who have distinguished themselves shows that more than 94% of them are doing work they like best. A man who doesn't enjoy his work seldom excels in it, no matter how hard he tries."

Success is as personal as your own toothbrush. It may lie in a business of your own. It may lie in working in a large company or in a small one. It may lie in selling or in administration or in invention or in accounting or in trouble-shooting other people's troubles. Only be sure that when you say—*THIS is what I want out of life*—the decision is yours.

Many sections of the Parker Prosperity Program help you decide what you want, where you are going. No matter how many efforts you have made toward finding this out—fill in the form below and think about it.

1. *What have I accomplished in life so far?*
   (a) Business-wise
   (b) Personally
   (c) Socially

2. *What would I like to accomplish in the future?*
   (a) In the business world
   (b) For my family
   (c) For myself (special projects or hobbies)

3. *What requirements will it take to accomplish each of the goals in Section Two?*
   (a) Those I have
   (b) Those I lack

Any *experience* you lack, you can find waiting for you somewhere. Go and get it.

Any *schooling* you lack is waiting in the right school or in the right book or correspondence course. Go get it.

The *time* you may lack, you can make up out of other time.

The *energy* you may lack—you don't lack. Just stir it up.

The *drive* you may lack is waiting right inside you; just waiting to be told where you want to go.

Psycho-Emotive Reminders:

Every success counselor sees that success depends on knowing what you want out of life—yet, out of 3,000 people interviewed, only about two per cent could say what they wanted. Tomorrow-itis keeps us from implementing our desires even when we know them. Take notice of how many times you use certain "tomorrow-itis" phrases, and see if you have the disease.

Question yourself also about your own indifference. You may feel indifferent to success in some field because it is not the field which really means *success* to you. On the other hand, your seeming indifference may come from fear which keeps you from taking action. Bring your fears into the open and they will not seem so strong. A great foe of fear and tomorrow-itis is the habit of *doing it now*, which you lift to higher and higher levels of accomplishment.

Where do you find the time? An analysis of an average worker's time shows many hours which can be displaced from unimportant or time-wasting pursuits. Even an extra hour a day gives you time to develop important new opportunities. Where do you find the energy? You have it, and only need to focus it. First get rid of anti-energy phrases and attitudes. Get rid of false ideas about what big jobs "take out of you." Realize your energy needs only to be stirred up.

An experiment in sleep opens a gold mine of time and energy. Most people think they need more sleep than they really need. A simple and exciting experiment shows you how much sleep YOU need, and gives you valuable insight into your energy patterns. You can go on to "push-ahead" any fatigue periods until you push a great deal of fatigue out of your life. Fill out a simple chart, think about it, and you'll have a picture of your accomplishments in the past, your accomplishments to come— and what you are going to do to make sure of those desired accomplishments.

My Personal Notes on Lesson Eight:

Suggestions:

Make more inventory-lists to help you know yourself better. List experiences you have had which taught you lessons about tomorrow-itis, about indifference, about "having time" and "having energy."

Make a list of your successes and a parallel list which shows the major factor that caused the success.

In regard to your goals, think of some unconventional ways you might reach them. One or more of these ways may suggest a new approach.

Check yourself on underlining key phrases in the text. often a word or two will trigger an entire train of valuable thought—and the same word or two can do this again and again.

The next and final lesson revolves around one significant fact: *Everything you get in life, you get from the people around you.* Here is the secret of personal magnetism—the final "plus quality" that helps you attract, influence and beneficially control other people—an exciting new formula that gives you million-dollar personality appeal.

How to Develop
a Million Dollar Personality

Straightforward Methods That Set Up
Your Success With People

EVERYTHING YOU GET IN LIFE, YOU get from the people around you.

Think about that for a moment, and you will realize how true it is. On the job, you get your raises, promotions, bonuses, great opportunities from *people*. In your private life, all the really important things—love, friendship, a harmonious family life—come from *people*.

And the major way you affect the people in your life is through your personality. The way they think of you, the way they react to you, the way they are influenced by you, the way they prefer

181

to help you or prefer to ignore you—depend somewhat on circumstances but mostly on personality.

That's why it pays so well to back up your prosperity power with personality power. J. V. Cerney, who gives you the secrets of a Million Dollar Personality, has been a doctor, a teacher, a sports coach, and now finds his greatest success as president of a consultant firm in human engineering. He gives you the secrets of personal magnetism which draw people to you. He shows you how to set up an endless number of willing partners who help you win the best in life.

Personality is social seduction

You may never have thought of it that way, but that is the way it is. It is with our personalities that we woo others into going our way. It is with personality, far more often than with logic, that we find help when we need it and get mighty boosts toward our goals.

With all that, a million dollar personality contains as much *give* as *take*. It has to! The person who overdoes the *take* side of his personality soon finds he isn't getting much from other people because he makes them feel *taken*.

Here is a check list. Go through it quickly. When you have recorded your *Yes* or *No* for each point—use good, black check-marks —go back and see where you showed *give* in your personality and where you showed *take*.

Some points, such as the first, will make you pause. This is purposeful. It calls your attention to the fact that so much depends on your approach.

GIVE or TAKE Estimation Scale

Yes No

— — I am determined to succeed.

— — I have goals toward which I am working.

— — I never boast about my accomplishments.

Yes No

— — I am classified as a "slick operator" in my work.

— — Anger, at times, controls my intelligence.

— — Courtesy is one of my virtues.

— — I take pride in being respectful.

— — I try to eliminate my offensive factors.

— — I accept criticism profitably.

— — I confess my faults without ulterior motive.

— — I blame only myself for my failures.

— — I will willingly accept help to improve myself.

— — I try to set a good example at all times.

— — I don't tolerate bad habits.

— — I try to see myself as others see me.

— — I find pleasure in living.

— — Life is no longer a race for dollars.

— — I have found dignity in my work.

— — I work to improve my mentality.

— — I read new material constantly.

— — Criticism no longer bothers me.

— — Contentment is mine.

— — I am full of controlled ambition.

— — I'll do anything worthwhile to fulfill ambition.

— — I am original in what I am now doing.

— — New ideas fascinate me. I put them to work.

— — I have no time for mental laziness.

— — I look for new and improved methods and no longer follow beaten paths.

— — I listen and take advice.

— — I draw no racial or religious lines.

— — I have plenty of energy to get things done.

— — I let my enthusiasm show.

— — I drive continuously for physical fitness.

— — I am usually happy.

— — I never harbor resentment.

— — Being cheerful is inexpensive.

— — I have no sour thoughts any more.

Yes No

— — I never repeat an unhappy incident.

— — I avoid everything worrisome and sad.

— — I can go to sleep peacefully anywhere.

— — Irritations no longer distract me.

— — I can concentrate on matters taking thought.

— — I can carry a job all the way through.

— — I am constantly looking for better methods.

— — I have many interests outside my job.

— — Show me my weakness and I'll improve.

— — I never gripe when others advance and I don't.

— — I don't accuse unless I have all the facts.

— — I always reason matters out carefully.

— — I never make "snap diagnoses" or "hot guesses."

— — I praise and revere those who inspire me.

— — I publicly praise those who merit it.

— — I am kind to everyone.

— — I always say thanks for help received.

— — I continuously fight the act of being selfish.

— — I seek only the best company and advice.

You need not score yourself. But observe yourself

While you score yourself several times in the Parker Prosperity Program, you need not look for any score on the GIVE and TAKE Estimation Scale. Observe yourself, however, as the Scale reflects your personality.

You have a pretty good idea as to which traits should have been checked *Yes* to indicate constructive social seduction. Any honest person knows where those *Yeses* should come in. The only question is—what to do about developing the qualities that add up to a million dollar personality—and what to do about squelching those that subtract.

Enthusiasm—your passport to a million-dollar personality

Every personality factor affects every other. Some personality factors carry others along with them—and *enthusiasm* carries along and strengthens so many of the good factors that it is indispensable.

Enthusiasm is human relations in "living color." Enthusiasm is the most catching of all emotions. Enthusiasm spells out confidence and self-reliance. It is warmth, friendliness and charm coupled to a working program—and above all, enthusiasm is *the* best method of getting people to think your way.

> A sales manager spent six months in testing and improving the presentation for his product, and working up a gorgeous brochure in full color. His product was honest and the price was right—but his problem was to get people to look at what he had to sell, since it was building lots on a West Indian island. His salesmen had to sell people first on the idea of taking a trip to this island—some 1500 miles from Miami—and looking around to see if they wanted to live there.
>
> When the presentation was *right,* the sales manager sent his force into the field. Some of his men and women did very well. Others, using the same presentation, got nowhere. What was the difference? Careful analysis showed it was *enthusiasm* or lack of enthusiasm on the salesperson's part. It was *enthusiasm* projected to a prospective buyer that made him put down a refundable deposit, then get onto a plane or a ship.

This is far more than just another story about enthusiasm as a selling force. Let us examine farther.

Some of the unsuccessful salespeople complained that the "pitch" was too long and left them worn out; but the enthusiastic (and successful) sellers never grew tired. *Enthusiasm conquers fatigue.*

The bulk of the prospects were older folk, ready for retirement. Many of the unsuccessful salespeople complained they couldn't "warm up" those suspicious old couples who clung to their stocks and bonds and took refuge behind their hearing aids. The enthusiastic salespeople, however, had no such trouble. *Enthusiasm conquers suspicion*—and *enthusiasm makes others WANT to communicate with you.*

Salesmen who had spent years in real estate were outsold by enthusiastic salesmen who were dealing in real estate for the first time. *Enthusiasm makes others overlook small shortcomings.*

The percentage of deals finally closed when enthusiastic salesmen got them rolling was far higher than the percentage closed when a non-enthusiastic salesmen did manage to get a couple to go down to "Retirement Island." The closings on the spot were handled by the sales manager himself, so all salesmen got equal treatment—but obviously the warm-up had a lot to do with the closing. *Enthusiasm leaves friendliness and trust behind it.*

Again, the enthusiastic salesmen won a far greater percentage of references—even when they did not secure deposits. Often when they could not sell to a couple, they sold to that couple's recommended friends. *Enthusiasm makes people willing to link their names to yours.*

Forget selling for a moment and look at what enthusiasm does:

Enthusiasm conquers your fatigue
Enthusiasm conquers suspicion in others
Enthusiasm makes others want to communicate with you
Enthusiasm makes others overlook your small shortcomings
Enthusiasm not only creates instant friendliness and trust, but also leaves friendliness and trust behind it
Enthusiasm makes others willing to link their names to yours

All this without regard to selling!—although it certainly helps to sell. You are not a salesman? You may live longer! But remember this, which so many people never seem to realize: In any kind of success, there is always a large element of *selling yourself.*

That is what makes enthusiasm social seduction in a nutshell, and the universal touchstone of good human relations.

The eight major ingredients of enthusiasm; try them on for size

1. Honestly want to know people. The introvert does not start with a desire to know people; he tends to avoid people. But an honest try at getting to know people soon shows him there is nothing painful in the process—and so much that is rewarding, it pays to stay out of your shell. Simply show you are interested in people. And to show your interest, demonstrate your interest. Give!

2. *Do things.* Get around! Enjoy the world's wealth of wonderful sights, sounds and experiences. Don't just stand by, watching—get in there and participate. Don't emphasize any dull and gray experience that may be forced upon you; do emphasize the bright and gay experiences you seek out. The more you seek out happy experience, the more it comes to you, and the more bright and gay is your life-pattern.

3. *Realize everyone has enthusiasm and the more he uses it, the stronger it gets.* Has your enthusiasm grown rusty? Give it some practise and it will gleam and glow. Bring it right out where everyone can see it. How long since you *believed* in something and sounded off about your enthusiastic belief? You don't have to wait till you find some mighty issue. Believe out loud that a movie is entertaining! Believe out loud that a flower is pretty! Practise your enthusiasm and it begins to swing and sing.

4. *Turn enthusiasm on even when you don't feel like it.* This harks back to role-playing. It has values within values, for it shows you how much control we exercise over our states of mind when we *want* to exercise that control. So turn on your enthusiasm even when you don't feel like it—and lo, you *are* enthusiastic! You turn off doubt. You turn off unhappiness. You bring in energy. You build interest and then interest on top of the interest till you have enthusiastic interest, the kind that counts. Find a time of the day when you tend to sag—such as the end of a day's work—and choose that time to turn on the enthusiasm.

Q: But won't it be merely a pose?

A: *Only for the first few seconds. Thought, state-of-being and action are all interwoven. When you act enthusiastic, in a moment you feel enthusiastic; and when you feel enthusiastic, you are enthusiastic, with full-scale power to communicate your enthusiasm to others.*

5. *Feed your interest with challenges that help you achieve.* An enthusiastic person finds it fun to keep a step ahead of himself, so to speak. He joyfully sets up challenges that carry him on. He enthusiastically maintains a state of constructive and happy dis-

satisfaction with the *status quo*. He loves challenges because he loves to succeed.

6. *Widen your horizons. Look beyond your work.* The mind will encompass endless interests. You need not run after everything that glitters, but you can see to it that something better than groaning exhaustion fills your leisure hours—and you'll return to your work more refreshed.

7. *Do what you enjoy doing.* Enthusiastic people take care of duties they don't enjoy—yet always find more in life to enjoy than the non-enthusiastic. Part of the secret is to look for what you enjoy and enthusiastically go to it. You may wait a long time if you unenthusiastically wait for it to come to you.

8. *Vary your routine.* Set up a "tomorrow schedule" in which you plan to do something new. Then do it and feel enthusiasm flow in. Keep an "anticipation pad" at your bedside to hold enthusiastic new ideas that come to you in the night. Jot down those ideas before they get away from you.

Is enthusiasm all you need for a million dollar personality?

No! We put that long list early in this lesson to make sure of that point. Enthusiasm with nothing behind it rings hollow. With *give* behind it, with *honesty* and *cooperation* behind it, with *willingness to work* behind it—enthusiasm becomes the major ingredient of a personality that brings success.

How to communicate with others, the "million dollar" way

Here is a conversation questionnaire. Check off *Yes* or *No* honestly, even if it hurts, right down the line. Again, you don't have to give yourself a formal score. But again, go back and think about the questions. They concern "talk"—but see how much more lies behind them. These questions help you see why your conversation is you.

Conversation Questionnaire

	Yes	No
1. Do I monopolize conversation?	—	—

Yes No

2. Do I think myself charming? .... — —
3. Can I talk a little nonsense too? ....— —
4. Do I insist on talking about matters of which I know
   very little? .... — —
5. Do I admit I don't know a lot of things? .... — —
6. Do I value the opinion of others? .... — —
7. Do I avoid slang? .... — —
8. Is my grammar poor? .... — —
9. Do I talk about the weather? .... — —
10. Does my education show? .... — —
11. Must I appear brilliant all the time? .... — —
12. Do I talk continuously? .... — —
13. Do I find relief in talking a lot? .... — —
14. Do I talk very little? .... — —
15. Do I talk about myself all the time? .... — —
16. Is the world wrong? .... — —
17. Is *my* opinion always right? .... — —
18. Am I sensitive to the feelings of others? .... — —
19. Do I listen to myself talk and enjoy it? .... — —
20. Do I tell only clean jokes? .... — —
21. Do I know when to shut up? .... — —
22. Have I ever learned to listen? .... — —
23. Am I considered a "big mouth"? .... — —
24. Do I smother angry words? .... — —
25. Do others like to confide in me? .... — —
26. Do I look people in the eye when talking? .... — —
27. Do I forget their names? .... — —
28. Is my disinterest in others apparent? .... — —
29. Do I walk away from gossip and slander? .... — —
30. Do I tend to monopolize conversations? .... — —
31. Do I tell my troubles to everyone? .... — —
32. Do I keep repeating the same lectures? .... — —
33. Do I discuss my family only when asked? .... — —
34. Do I stutter or have pronunciation problems? ...... — —
35. Do I express my thoughts clearly? .... — —

You've taken a little while to think about the questionnaire and your answers? You have, we hope, underlined any point here (or elsewhere) that has special meaning to you? Then let's go on:

How to make your conversation project your best personality and do more for you

1. Speak with expression. What you say is important, and most people stop there. Remember that *how* you say it is very important. To prove this, close your eyes and listen to a few people speak— preferably people you don't know. Then you'll see how much the expression of the voice has to do with your impression of the personality.

You may be too shy to dramatize what you have to say. Try it— it is not resented, it is appreciated! Show interest. Show excitement. Speak slowly for emphasis. Speak more rapidly when you sum up several points already explained. Keep the tone of your voice up where it can be heard and act out what you say with appropriate expression—and watch people listen to you. Watch your personality get across.

2. Hear yourself as others hear you. Try listening to yourself for a change. A ten-dollar tape recorder can give you a million dollar improvement in your conversation. Do you articulate your words or slur them? Do you fail to use your jaw, your lips and your tongue in speaking, as so many do? (Words were not meant to slide out of your face; they are meant to be well and truly *spoken.*)

One man said: "I was amazed to find that I had picked up some annoying vocal mannerisms from a certain TV pitchman. And he's someone I don't like!"

Hear yourself as others hear you, and keep on making recordings until you hear yourself as a likeable, personable person—the way you want to be heard.

3. Talk technically to technicians only. This is not the same as saying: *Speak in simple words*—but it's close to that generally good advice. You should not ever "talk down" to anybody. But "talk his language." Bear in mind it may not be your language. There are plenty of people who talk your language, unless you are very unusual. Save your specialized talk for them.

4. Be an enthusiastic listener. Part of conversation? A very vital part! As you know, everybody likes to be recognized in some manner. Recognize him, then, for what *he* has to say. And show by your expression, by an occasional word of understanding, by an occasional short question which can be quickly answered, that you really are "with him." He'll like you for it. And on your side—you may find out you have a lot to learn!

5. Give the other fellow credit. Try consciously to put some kind of *credit* into your next conversation. This too is part of recognition. Compliments are always welcome when they are justified. Recognition of something special about the other fellow puts a glow into his heart; tell him you know he is the fellow who . . . etc.

6. Agree more than you disagree. Indeed, with practise, you'll find it possible never really to disagree, and so never set up conflict.

This does not mean you should accept whatever you are told. But you can give the other fellow credit for being right in something, for making good sense, for ably demonstrating the other side of the question. And then you can go on to say what *you* think. Thus you put across what you want to say but you do not make the other person feel small.

7. Do not make any other person feel small. Take this as an over-all rule, no matter to whom you speak, no matter what you have to say.

8. Talk about the other person's interests. This makes him want to listen to you. It is social wooing of considerable power. Moreover, most people will talk about their own interests—once you've started them off—for only a certain length of time before they realize it. Then they'll hand over the conversation to you, to show they are courteous, and the floor is yours for what *you* have to say.

9. Ask for advice. People like to do favors, especially when they are quickly done and don't cost anything. A person who has given you advice feels kindly toward you.

10. Learn the other fellow's name and use it. This is universal good advice in personal relations. Everybody knows it, yet often it is neglected. But when you learn the other fellow's name and use his name in speaking to him, you go far toward making a friend.

How to avoid emotional traps and keep on expanding your personality

Emotional traps are all social; or they should be. As you will see, however, they often shade over into business or professional life—because your personality is not limited to "social" contacts, and neither is the other fellow's.

What is an emotional trap? Broadly speaking, it is a topic with steel teeth. It is a topic you avoid as much as you can, because it bites. For example:

> Politics
> Religion
> Divorce or separation
> Sex (when it is irrelevant)
> Business (in the sense of prying)
> Someone else's choice of friends or associates (and generally
>   your own)
> Failure to achieve (anyone's)
> Mental capacity
> Your superiority
> Appearance
> Relatives
> Hereditary factors
> Very personal likes or dislikes
> Methods used by other people to gain attention
> Reminding a person of what you have done for him

Of course there are exceptions. Your own good judgment applies to everything in the Parker Prosperity Program. But remember the rule more than the exceptions: Stay out of emotional traps!

Expect, however, to see and hear them all around you. Take them as opportunities—because the way you handle other people's emotional traps can establish you, in their eyes, as a person of wonderful personality.

How to cope with emotional traps and turn them into assets

To put it another way: how do you avoid those steel teeth when another person snaps them right at you?

> A small-town newspaper editor remarked that he might have been lynched long ago if he had not learned how to handle people who pound his desk and demand to know his stand on controversial questions. He answers with another question, such as: "How you YOU feel about that question, Mr. Jones? What is YOUR opinion?" Then he listens with flattering attention till the storm has blown itself out.

This editor is liked and respected. Few of us are in so sensitive a spot as a small-town newspaper editor. When a controversial topic is thrown into your face, toss it back gracefully. (And notice the *recognition* this gives the other fellow!)

You should seldom, if ever, attempt to change any other person's mind on a topic he feels with deep emotion. Notice we say *feel*. He may not *know* very much, but it is his *feelings* that count. Whenever you become more interested in changing a person's mind than in winning his respect, you harm your own personality.

If you find you must have some outlet against a person who is overbearing, critical, nasty, or just plain mean, don't get "unglued" in his presence. Excuse yourself. Walk away. Go and wash your hands and face. Place cold water on the back of your neck. Return when you have recaptured your self-control—which always is evident in a million-dollar personality.

Then you are prepared to proceed without challenging the other person's self-respect, which is intensely important to him. And here's a way to catch him completely off-guard . . .

Nod. Seem to agree. Don't declare yourself in words. You may take the wind out of his sails completely. When it is obviously time for you to say *something*, you might ask him a question about some detail of what he has been saying and force him to think. *You do not agree in words*, in a ticklish situation, but you keep your influence intact by leading along the other fellow.

And that is what your million dollar personality is for—to influence others. You see, a good personality does really amount to social wooing.

Is there a way to predict how others will act, so you can avoid having trouble with them?

While there is no sure-fire way, a very good way is to *judge a person's probable reactions by his known fears.*

How do you know his fears unless you know the man very well? You often can make very close guesses.

Does he work in some area which is being threatened by a new technology? He fears that new technology and he will not like you for praising it.

Is he getting old? He will be sensitive to remarks, even if "not personal," about the powers and prerogatives of youth, about men "on their way up," and so forth. And no matter how able he may be, he'd rather not hear any talk about sexual potency.

Has he earned a couple of doctorates and is he going for another one, meanwhile doing little about earning a living? Avoid talking about people who fear facing the world, for that is an emotional sore toe you don't want to tread upon.

Does he hate some minority group? Then he fears them. Use your judgment.

Does he boast about his lack of formal education? Never mind your own doctorate. (Yes, there is a fear at work here. It is fear that he will be less well thought of because he never put a sheepskin on his wall. If he had a really solid personality, he would accept himself without boasting.)

Is he a martinet, a brute to his employees, a terror to his family? We have met him before; he is full of fears. Do not threaten his very shaky inner security.

But what about your own healthy ego?

In influencing people, in social wooing, you obviously go out of your way to please people. Is this going to erode your own ego till nothing is left?

The best answer is this: Find a person whom you admire for his success, his charm, his great circle of friends—and see if he has lost his ego.

You'll see he has plenty of ego. Of course he has ego, because he *believes in himself,* and this is the unshakable, solid-rock foundation of his million dollar personality.

Believe in yourself and your ego will pay you great dividends. You *can't* be an underdog.

Words cannot convey the difference between a man who stays out of arguments because he is a coward, and a man who stays out of arguments because he is strong enough not to argue. But other people feel that difference.

Words cannot convey the difference between a man who has built a circle of friends who share his hates—and a man whose friends share his love of humanity. But humanity feels the difference.

To know where you are going is to believe in yourself. Know this.

To prepare well to get where you want to go is to have faith in yourself. Show that faith.

To handle problems in a positive way, rather than letting them floor you, is to show your belief in your own capabilities. Show that belief.

To find the world full of sights, sounds, events and people worth being enthusiastic about is to show you are a constructive person. Show your constructiveness.

And don't worry about your ego. *Believe in yourself,* take notice of what makes a million dollar personality, and you can have a million dollar personality. And you can have all the happiness and success that goes with it.

Your human-relations IQ

How would you stand up under the following test if someone else filled it out? Stand off and see yourself. Check the entries. *This time, calculate your score.* If it's above 165, you either wear a halo or did not answer honestly. If under 100, you need serious work on your personality. If between 100 and 150, you are basically all right and a million dollar personality is not far out of your grasp. Between 150 and 165—you almost have it.

	15 points	√	10 points	√	5 points	√
Appearance	Professional, neat, clean		Non-professional but adequate		Careless, dirty, slovenly	
Confidence	Self-assured		Competent but can't express himself		Can't make decisions; apologetic	
Countenance	Pleasant, assured, sympathetic		Poker-faced		Unpleasant, annoyed	
Friendliness	Exudes warmth and friendliness		Kind, but slightly aloof		Cold, impassive, unsympathetic	
Judgment	Decisive, authoritative but friendly		Decision without friendliness		Unbalanced, thoughtless	
Manners	Pleasant, well-mannered		So-so		Nasty, ill-bred	
Mannerisms	None		Minor		Offensive	
Poise	Excellent		Balanced		Reacts badly to everything	
Speech	Clean		Average		Inarticulate, crude, offensive	
Understanding	Quick to comprehend		Grasps an idea		Dull	
Voice	Modulated, friendly, charming, cultivated		Normal		Aggravating	
	Subtotal		Subtotal		Subtotal	
			Grand TOTAL			

Personality is man-made

You were not born with a personality. In your younger years, other people formed your personality—so personality always is man-made. But you have arrived at years in which YOU can change and vastly improve your personality. *Within you is everything you need for success.* Within you is enthusiasm, drive, ambition, kindliness, courage, cooperation—everything, including your own good common sense.

Use that last factor to make yourself know how important it is to have a good personality. Then take the rest and build your own place in the sun.

Psycho-Emotive Reminders:

Because you influence others through the power of your personality, your personality greatly influences what you get out of life. Personality is social seduction, which woos others into going our way; but a million dollar personality contains as much give as take.

Enthusiasm is the passport to a successful personality. Enthusiasm conquers fatigue, creates friendliness and trust, makes others overlook shortcomings; it is social seduction in a nutshell. To become enthusiastic, honestly want to know people, get out and change your routines, turn on your faith and belief at low periods, feed your interest with challenges that help you achieve. Only be sure that solid human qualities back up your enthusiasm.

Your conversation can project your best personality. Speak with drama and expression. Find a way to listen to yourself and thus improve your "talking personality." Be an enthusiastic listener, give the other fellow lots of credit, agree more than you disagree. Avoid falling into emotional traps, and turn enemies into friends by the way you handle emotional traps in others.

You often can guess what another person fears, and you can judge his reactions accordingly. When you attempt to please others you need not hurt your own healthy ego. The great key to a healthy ego and an all-around good personality is: Believe in yourself. Show this, and others will see it. Calculate your human-relations IQ and you will see that most people have what it takes to build a million-dollar personality. Personality is man-made, and you can start building your own success in human relations right now.

My Personal Notes on Lesson Nine:

Suggestions:

Check other people's personalities on the Give or Take Estimation Scale, the Conversation Questionnaire, the list of emotional traps, and the human-relations IQ chart. This greatly increases your insight into human nature.

Notice the relation of personality to mood. There are times when you and every other person find it particularly hard to be pleasant. What causes those times? What can you do about it?

Make your own list of what enthusiasm does for people. Notice enthusiasm at work in business, personal and sport situations.

Take special notice of the way in which people see *personality* more than they see *person*. Check this tendency in yourself to see how true it is. Think back to the "face of the personality" in a previous chapter.

Notice how your goals in life are really an expression of your personality, and change as your personality develops.

There are no further lessons in the Parker Prosperity Program. Go on to check your improved Prosperity Quotient.

PROSPERITY QUOTIENT ANALYSIS

As with the other Prosperity Quotient Analyses, this final analysis is designed to:

1. Test your receptivity to the ideas and methods set forth in the Parker Prosperity Program
2. Emphasize certain key ideas or psycho-emotive motifs

This final analysis scans through the entire Program, but most of the questions which follow are keyed to the last three Lessons.

Instructions:

Answer *Yes* or *No* to each of the following questions. Be true to yourself—don't try to guess the answer—and do not change your answer after you have checked it. Remember this is *your* private record.

Where a question is really a statement, let your "Yes" or "No" indicate whether you agree or disagree. Statement-questions, changes of pace and other devices are used to accustom you to reading and thinking accurately. Look up any word you may not understand.

Scoring instructions are given at the end of the quiz.

	Yes	No
1. If you don't like your outward face, you never can like your inward "face."	—	—
2. Should you let other people know you like them?	—	—
3. To get rid of tomorrow-itis, put off everything until tomorrow.	—	—
4. It pays to see how much sleep you really need.	—	—
5. For the sake of your ego, should you shout down anyone who does not agree with you?	—	—
6. Does your enthusiasm make others notice all your small shortcomings?	—	—
7. Can you use emotional appeal only on people who are very emotional?	—	—
8. Ideas you reject, when you try to think of a good idea,		

have nothing to do with eventually finding that good idea. — —

9. Inherent in our autonomous powers is the capability for physiological aggrandizement through psychological equanimity. — —

10. Although you make progress by going forward, you should stop all progress as soon as you make a mistake. — —

11. Should you ever obligate yourself to another person promising to have something done by a certain date? — —

12. A person who wants to make a good impression should keep all drama out of his voice. — —

13. Do we often tend to find reasons why we *must* be right—whether we are right or wrong? — —

14. A man at a meeting should attempt to have an answer for everything, in the hope that now and then he'll be right. — —

15. Can a scrapbook do more for you than remind you of recent events? — —

16. Must a definite goal in life be attained before you are forty? — —

17. Can the way you speak reveal your own opinion of your own store of energy? — —

18. Nobody can help his success by playing the role of success. — —

19. The instructions received by your "inner steersman" are built into you at birth. — —

20. Any knowledge you gather may relate itself to any knowledge previously gathered. — —

21. Is it worth your while to have lunch with successful people? — —

22. The "feeling of success" has nothing to do with success. — —

23. Is there any connection between the optimism you feel and the success you win? — —

Yes No

24. Everything you get out of life you get from the people around you. — —

25. When anyone expresses a *hate,* he generally expresses a *fear*—which helps you know him. — —

26. Counselors are rarely if ever asked: "How can I make more money?" — —

27. Unless you always take and never give, you'll never have money. — —

28. The death rate among high-salaried people is considerably higher than among the low-salaried. — —

29. By pushing back your fatigue times, you can push a great deal of fatigue out of your life. — —

30. Have you ever asked this question and answered it firmly: "What have I accomplished in life?" — —

31. Should you try to "speak the other fellow's language" in conversing with him? — —

32. Most people don't know how capable they really are. — —

33. Do you build upon your successes, rather than upon your failures? — —

34. In an hour a day you can find out a great deal about any business. — —

35. Will your subconscious mind accept any idea you consistently and strongly give it? — —

36. Once you have a firm belief, should you not hold onto it forever, rather than examining and re-evaluating it? — —

37. When you are too inhibited, you prevent yourself from making progress. — —

38. Do you ever make a promise to yourself—and keep it? — —

39. "Hold a picture of yourself long and steadily enough in your mind's eye and you will be drawn toward it." Do you agree? — —

40. Is there a strong relation between imagination and reality? — —

41. Do you downgrade your attitudes of prosperity when

Yes No

you generally find fault with successful people?   — —

42. Do you realize that it is possible to change your mind about yourself?   — —

43. Is jealousy in marriage generally caused by self-doubt?   — —

44. Can you make good use of the gambling instinct by "betting on yourself"?   — —

45. Have you found a job you really like?   — —

46. Agreeing that when you know what you want out of life it makes you no *smarter*—do you agree it makes you far more *effective*?   — —

47. Does this make sense to you? "You are not so much a human being as you are a human becoming."   — —

48. Do you believe that, by and large, nothing can stop you except yourself?   — —

49. Do you believe that beliefs which hold you back can be swept away by beliefs which propel you forward?   — —

50. Do you believe you are going to be prosperous and successful?   — —

Here's how to rate your answers:
The following questions should have been answered Yes:

1, 2, 4, 9, 11, 13, 15, 17, 20, 21, 23, 24, 25, 29, 30, 31, 32, 33, 34, 35, 38, 39, 40, 41, 42, 43, 44, 45, 46, 47, 48, 49, 50.
All others, *No.*

Now score yourself, allowing two points for each question answered correctly. Allow no score for questions answered incorrectly or for questions not answered.

Record your Prosperity Quotient below.

My Prosperity Quotient has risen to ————————

Summary and Final Message

YOU MAY CONFIDENTLY EXPECT your Prosperity Quotient to rise all during your productive life. As your prosperity grows stronger, so does your potential for even greater prosperity grow stronger.

As you build your Palace of Prosperity, keep on coming back to this book to check again on *what prosperity is made of.* Especially, re-read the portions you have annotated and underlined. Read your notes through, add to them what experience has taught you; then re-read again a few months later. Thus you reinforce the habits that build your Palace of Prosperity on a mighty foundation. *You keep on reminding yourself of what prosperity is made of.*

And when you come right down to it, what is the main ingredient of any man's prosperity?

Himself.

YOURself—glowing with illimitable forces—sparked by a prosperity potential that really cannot be measured because it is so big.

Have you noticed how everything in this Program points to

YOU as architect and builder and custodian of your own prosperity?

First of all, you became acquainted with the great law that says: *You must give before you can get.* You saw how other laws, such as the prosperity law of command and the prosperity law of vacuum build on the first great law. The law of imaging gave you the keystone thought of GOAL so that you are constantly able to reinforce it.

In the next Lesson you found a reaffirmation of the great truth: *We are rich or poor, not because of God, but because of the way in which we use the human qualities God gave us.* You saw how a positive mental attitude leads to motivations of prosperity and to actions that bring prosperity even where others fail. You learned great secrets of enthusiasm, and how goals can be won by transferring a positive mental attitude from one person to another.

You were then introduced to a positive technique for freeing the latent powers of your mind—the simple art of self-hypnosis. You read how to gain instant relief from much nervous tension, and how to lift yourself onto a strong and cheerful level of self-confidence—which of course is the level on which you do your best work. You also received significant aid in breaking habits you want to break, and saw how self-hypnosis can get rid of fatigue and give you great new floods of energy.

You went on to examine five simple actions, easily within your power, which give you a directed personal drive that breaks through barriers. You know how to cast out any thought that you can't get what you want; how to generate dozens of money-making ideas; how to make your income take you where you want to go; how to multiply your performance by the power of ten; how to use leverage to move your world. It became apparent that you can increase your effectiveness right now, in your present setup, almost overnight.

You proceeded, and learned the power of emotional appeal and the few simple techniques that put that power in your hands. The fatal four emotional appeals—self-preservation, money, romance and recognition—lose their mystery and become instant tools of persuasion and personal influence. They also stand behind your own influence upon *yourself* in clearing your mind of distraction, helping you sleep better, handling life's situations constructively, building your prosperity day by day, hour by hour.

You moved on to a practical consideration of your subconscious mind as a partner in your prosperity. You took firm hold of the natural talent that channels the subconscious away from failure and always toward success. You saw that your subconscious does not reason—it accepts—but once it accepts your drive toward riches, it works through your conscious mind to give you the life you desire. You reach the "Mother Lode" of your subconscious mind and take hold of a driving force almost beyond imagination.

Going on, you found out that your inward "face" means more to your prosperity than does your physical, shaving-mirror face. A kind of "mental surgery" enables you to change the inward "face" which is your true personality. You get in touch with your invisible "steersman" who is waiting for the *right* orders and the *right* goal. A natural guidance system now corrects your errors, turns any error into a renewed great impetus in driving forward.

Proceeding with increased understanding of your own potential, you reinforced your understanding of the mighty touchstone of prosperity—*knowing what you want out of life*. Dynamic thinking became a great new habit that always sustains you. With this new way of thinking you can do more than you ever thought possible, feel fine on less sleep, make every working minute worth more and get more fun and relaxation out of your leisure. Big jobs no longer "take it out of you," but rather propel you ever-upward in fields where you know you do your best.

The final Lesson showed you how to develop all the great qualities wrapped up in "a million-dollar personality." You realized that everything you get in life, you get from people around you. Secrets of communicating with others now make sure they *want* to go your way. You project the prosperity-building part of yourself, avoid falling into emotional traps, instantly see ways in which to control and influence others. You still are *giving* to others— mightily—but you get immensely more than you give; and you, they and the whole fabric of society is benefited.

It's up to YOU, beyond the shadow of a doubt. And if ever you thought it takes a superman to win the life of his dearest dreams, now you know better. It does take work. It does take patience. But it does *not* take any quality YOU don't have—so long as you see it, believe in it, use it!

Somewhere in the back of his mind, every man carries a plan for his Palace of Prosperity. Take out that dusty blueprint. Clean it up. Modernize it. Plan for a Palace that is broader and longer and higher and finer than any you ever planned before. And now—right now—*start building!*